Economics for Christian Homeschoolers

Scott Clifton

Copyright © 2022-2023, Scott Clifton.
All rights reserved.

ISBN: 9798356447587

LIVE ONLINE CLASSES
High School and College Credits
ENGLISH & HISTORY

Online Christian-Worldview High School College Credit Opportunity! Families interested in their high schoolers earning dual enrollment credits online should take a look at Home School Partners.

Home School Partners offers online, Christian-worldview high school English and History classes. Students can earn 30 credits through a nationally accredited university.

The weekly, 50-minute, live online classes are taught by Scott Clifton, M.Ed. Scott has been a homeschool co-op instructor and director since 2002; he is also an author and the father of six homeschool graduates. He offers a hands-on class approach, with structure, interaction, discussion, and fun. The classes' foundation is a pro-limited-government, pro-free-market, Christian worldview, and students learn how to express and defend this perspective.

Here's a chance to get your student 30 college credits in high school without sacrificing a Christian worldview!

Western Civilization I • Western Civilization II
American Government and Politics
U.S. History I • U.S. History II
Civics • Economics • World Literature
American Literature • British Literature
Composition I • Composition II

Register now!

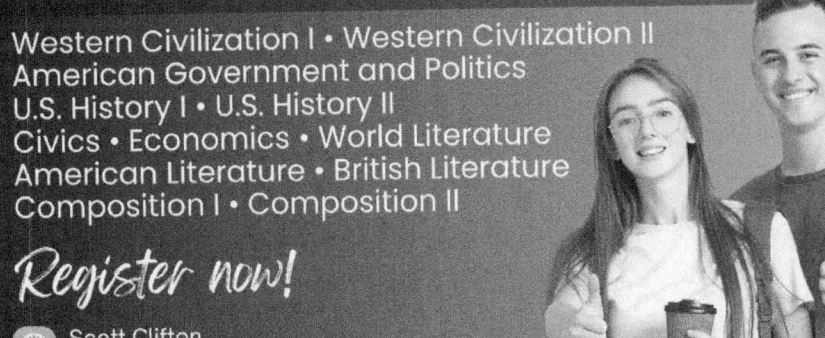

Scott Clifton
www.homeschoolpartners.net/online

Table of Contents • Weekly Reading Layout

WEEK 1	Day 1 – Economics Defined • Understanding Economics	1
	Day 2 – Living Outside of Normal Economics	4
	Day 3 – Should the Government Interfere in the Economy?	7
	Day 4 – CLAIM: "You Should <u>Have</u> to Give to the Poor!" • Quiz 1	11
WEEK 2	Day 1 – How To Use Man's Selfishness for Economic Good	12
	Day 2 – "The True Functions of Government"	15
	Day 3 – Camels, Needles, Moths, and Eagles	18
	Day 4 – CLAIM: "We Have to Stop Those Evil Robots!" • Quiz 2	23
WEEK 3	Day 1 – The Right to Property	25
	Day 2 – Economics Terms You Should Know	28
	Day 3 – What Is "Money"?	32
	Day 4 – Money, Weights, and Fraud • Quiz 3	34
WEEK 4	Day 1 – Test 1	37
	Day 2 – Profit: Not a Bad Word at All	37
	Day 3 – Capitalism: Mutual, Voluntary, and Beneficial	43
	Day 4 – Socialism, Part 1: Immoral and Anti-Christian	48
WEEK 5	Day 1 – Socialism, Part 2: Irrational and Unworkable	52
	Day 2 – "Why the Socialist State Is Impossible"	57
	Day 3 – The Broken Window	58
	Day 4 – The Broken-Window Fallacy and War • Quiz 4	62
WEEK 6	Day 1 – Test 2	64
	Day 2 – "Inflation in One Page"	64
	Day 3 – Inflation: Counterfeiting and Robbery	66
	Day 4 – The Federal Reserve: Stealing 97 Percent (So Far)	69
WEEK 7	Day 1 – CLAIM: "The Government Needs to Help Doctors!"	74
	Day 2 – Prices, Price Controls, and "Price Gouging"	75
	Day 3 – Grocery Stores and the DMV	79
	Day 4 – "I, Pencil" • Quiz 5	80

WEEK 8	Day 1 – Government Spending and Waste	85
	Day 2 – The Curse of Bureaucrats	90
	Day 3 – Public Works, Shovels, and Spoons	94
	Day 4 – CLAIM: "Monopolies Must Be <u>Stopped</u>!" • Quiz 6	96
WEEK 9	Day 1 – Test 3	97
	Day 2 – Unintended Consequences: Potatoes and Cobras	98
	Day 3 – Tariffs: Pickled Beets, Policies, and Plunder	101
	Day 4 – CLAIM: "You Support Greed and Selfishness!"	105
WEEK 10	Day 1 – Taxes and Exactions	106
	Day 2 – CLAIM: "Saving Money Hurts the Economy!"	110
	Day 3 – Answering Economic Fallacies, Part 1	112
	Day 4 – Not Very "Stimulating" At All • Quiz 7	113
WEEK 11	Day 1 – The Minimum Wage Mess	114
	Day 2 – Increasing Your Wages and Success at Work	120
	Day 3 – Labor Unions, Unequal Yoking, and Mammon	126
	Day 4 – Unintended Consequences, Part 2 • Quiz 8	130
WEEK 12	Day 1 – Test 4	131
	Day 2 – CLAIM: "Statistics <u>Prove</u> That Socialism Works!"	131
	Day 2 – CLAIM: "The <u>Government</u> Has to Build Roads!"	132
	Day 3 – "The Rich and the Poor: A Fairy Tale"	134
WEEK 13	Day 1 – Unintended Consequences, Part 3	138
	Day 2 – Answering Economic Fallacies, Part 2	139
	Day 3 – "The Luxury Tax Myth"	140
	Day 4 – CLAIM: "College Should Be <u>Free</u>!" • Quiz 9	141
WEEK 14	Day 1 – CLAIM: "We <u>Have</u> to Regulate Barbers!"	142
	Day 2 – Final Review, Part 1	143
	Day 3 – Final Review, Part 2	144
	Day 4 – Test 5 (Final)	145

What Kingdom Are You a Part Of?	147

How To Use This Book

Easy to Understand • Convenient • Self-Directed

Economics for Christian Homeschoolers is a one-semester (14-week) course for high schoolers. The layout is generally four sections per week: concise and focused on one topic. Each reading section is also topped off with questions to encourage students to think about each day's material. The book's sections/ chapters have titles such as "8.1 – Government Spending and Waste," which means that a student reads that section on Week 8, Day 1. (This book also includes references to quizzes and tests; these apply only to students in my in-person or online Economics class.)

Usually this is a second-semester study, with Civics the first semester; I teach that class in my in-person and online co-op classes using the book *Civics for Christian Homeschoolers* (see **homeschoolpartners.net/books**).

On my online and in-person co-op classroom days for Economics, we review the previous week's assignments; the other four days students finish the readings at home. Students who are *not* in my class can use a modified schedule—e.g., parents, you might assign your student one four-day reading schedule, then use "Day 5" to look over the review questions for those four days of readings. Or you could just each day look over that day's reading selection and review questions together. Of course, these are just suggestions—*you* know what works best for your family!

Students using this book should be able to, in most or nearly all cases, independently complete the daily readings and answer the review questions. If you'll visit homeschoolpartners.net/econkey, you'll find a free answer key to the review questions at the end of each of the daily readings.

American Government: The Other Early High School Area of Study

Whatever high school year your student completes this book, may I suggest that the next year you consider *American Government & Politics: A Christian Worldview*? (It's a one-semester or two-semester course; see the front of this book for details. You can find even more details at **homeschoolpartners.net**.)

Online College Credit Classes for High Schoolers

Would you like your homeschooled student to be able to earn 30 English and history college credits in high school—taught from a *Christian* worldview, instead of the "woke," anti-Christian perspective often taught at many local community colleges? If so, see **homeschoolpartners.net** (or the front of this book) for details. And if you have any questions about this book or the Civics, American Government, or literature sets for Christian homeschoolers, feel free to contact me on my web site (homeschoolpartners.net), and I'll do my best to help!

Many blessings,
Scott Clifton

1.1 – Economics Defined • Understanding Economics

Economics Defined

What is **economics**? Well, since we're approaching the subject from a Christian worldview, let's start by looking at the concept as the Bible describes it. In the twelfth chapter of the book of Luke, Jesus says many things, including these:

- It is foolish to pursue riches, instead of being *"rich toward God."*
- Trust God to provide for your food and clothing.
- Be ready for the return of Christ.
- Use your talents, money, and possessions to further God's kingdom.

Another way to express that last bullet is this way: "Be a good **steward** of what God gifts you with. A steward historically has been a manager of a household's affairs (finances, servants, and so on). Stewards were also responsible for training the oldest son of the owner of the estate, so that the son would be ready to run it after his father's death. One example of this is when Abram was still childless, before God had worked the great miracle of giving him a child in his and Sarah's old age, he had the following exchange with God in Genesis 15:1-2 (bold added):

> ...[T]he word of the LORD came unto Abram in a vision, saying, "Fear not, Abram: I am thy shield, and thy exceeding great reward." And Abram said, "LORD God, what wilt thou give me, seeing I go childless, and the **steward** of my house is this Eliezer of Damascus?"

Here Abram is saying that he has no child to make the steward of his household, except for a hired man. And after Jesus says those things in the above bullets, He has this fascinating exchange with Peter in Luke 12:41-44:

> Then Peter said unto him, "Lord, speakest thou this parable unto us, or even to all?" And the Lord said, "Who then is that faithful and wise steward, whom his lord shall make ruler over his household, to give them their portion of meat in due season? Blessed is that servant, whom his lord when he cometh shall find so doing. Of a truth I say unto you, that he will make him ruler over all that he hath."

Did you catch the word *steward* in that passage? Here's another look at the key part, this time with the Greek word in place of the word *steward* in bold:

"Who then is that faithful and wise οἰκονόμος...?"

If we *transliterate* that bolded word—in other words, if we convert the Greek letters in that word into the equivalent English letters and sounds—the passage looks like this (bold added again):

*"Who then is that faithful and wise **oikonomos**...?"*

If you pronounce that bold word, it sounds like *economics*, and, of course, the Greek word above is the origin of that English word. So stewardship—managing and using resources like money and property—is what economics is all about.[1] Early English definitions of the word *economy* centered around efficiently managing a home or business, including how money was spent. (The word *economy* is still often used as a synonym of the word *efficiency*.) Here's how Noah Webster, in his famous 1828 *American Dictionary of the English Language*, defined the word *economy*:

- ...[T]he management, regulation, and government of a family or the concerns of a household.
- The management of...the expenditure of money.
- A frugal [thrifty] and judicious [wise] use of money; that management which expends money to advantage, and incurs no waste...a prudent management of all the means by which property is saved or accumulated; a judicious application of time, of labor, and of the instruments of labor.[2]

For decades at many schools, young women took "Home Economics" classes. "Home Ec," as it was also called, focused on teaching them how to run a household. In other words, Home Ec classes gave those young ladies tips and practice on how to be a homemaker: topics like child raising, cooking, and "economizing"—saving money and spending it efficiently.

"You Can't <u>Possibly</u> Understand Economics!"

That's the kind of thing you often hear in today's world, where many of those in power regularly tell us to "Trust the Experts" (experts who agree with—and who are paid large salaries by—those in power) and "Trust the Science" (the "science" hyped by scientists who agree with—and who are paid large salaries by—those in power). Similarly, economics is often said to be too hard for anyone but The Experts to understand. That was the general vibe I got from both economics classes I took—one in high school, and one in college; both classes were loaded down with headache-inducing charts and graphs, and baffling terms like *long-term ophiological domestic marginal elasticity*. But let me point out two important things that you, the homeschooled young person, should keep in mind:

---

[1] Jesus also told a parable about an unjust and wasteful steward in Luke 16.
[2] *Webster's Dictionary 1828: American Dictionary of the English Language*, "Economy," https://webstersdictionary1828.com/Dictionary/economy.

1. Yes, you absolutely *can* understand economics.
2. No, you absolutely *cannot* understand economics.

First, to an extent, the basics of nearly *any* subject can be understood by nearly all those who want to learn it and are willing to put in a little time and effort. Part of this ability to understand different concepts—a sensible, Biblical view of the world—comes from a Christian's fear of and obedience to God:

> *The fear of the LORD is the beginning of wisdom: a good understanding have all they that do his commandments (Psalm 111:10).*

> *I understand more than the ancients, because I keep thy precepts [commandments] (Psalm 119:100).*

In that first verse, God's Word tells us that if we have a "fear of the LORD," we will begin to gain wisdom. And in the second verse, King David says that his understanding was greater than the old and wise, because he kept God's precepts. And it plays the other way, too; wickedness in the hearts and actions of individuals can cause them to become gullible and blinded to the truth—to be fooled more easily by lies:

> **Those who fear God, obey Him, and know His word will have a better understanding of many topics, including economics.**

> *A wicked doer giveth heed to false lips; and a liar giveth ear to a naughty tongue (Proverbs 17:4).*

Does that mean that all Christians will be experts on economics, able to successfully explain the meaning of terms like *long-term ophiological domestic marginal elasticity* to, say, a group of toddlers?

Well, that's doubtful. If you tried to explain that term to a group of toddlers closely gathered around you, they would likely start crying, and probably drench your shoes with tears or drool (or worse).

But a Christian who reads and obeys God's Word has a much greater chance of successfully understanding what makes the world tick, the nature of mankind and how he acts in this world, and what economic decisions the public will probably make in response to this or that government policy.

Second, no doubt even the most brilliant person of all time couldn't even come close to having a complete understanding of economics—that is, the area of economics that attempts to grasp how the many millions of individuals work in a nation, and the many billions of daily decisions they make on how they earn, spend, save, and manage their money and other property.

A steward's job of managing the economics of just *one* household is a full-time job.

Full.

Time.

Job.

> *Even the most brilliant person ever can't come close to grasping how millions of individuals work, spend, save, and manage their money.*

So how could anyone develop the strange notion that he has the ability—or the moral right—*to direct the buying and selling within an entire neighborhood, city, county, state, or nation*? It is arrogant and irrational for someone to believe this, but you probably won't be surprised to learn that some individuals actually think that they have this magical ability. Even worse, they also believe—by a very strange coincidence—that they have the right *to impose their plans upon everybody else.*

But economics is a useful study, though we can't know *everything*, because we can analyze *results* of economic policies and predict results of new or potential economic policies. To help us make these predictions, it's vital to understand how mankind acts, based on what the Bible and (to a lesser extent) real-life experiences and history tell us.

What Do You Think?

1. Look up Proverbs 28:5 and Titus 1:7. What do these verses say to back up two of the main points of today's reading?
2. Define *economics*, *steward*, and *home economics*.
3. How does knowing and keeping God's Word make a person wiser?
4. Explain the difference between the job of a steward and an attempt by a politician to direct a nation's economy.
5. Fill in the blanks to finish these passages: "The fear of the LORD is the ___: a good ___ have all they that do his commandments" (Psalm 111:10); "I understand more than the ancients, because I ___" (Psalm 119:100).

1.2 – Living Outside of Normal Economics

The Bible is not a science textbook. But that doesn't mean that it is incorrect on the scientific matters it addresses. Likewise, neither is the Bible an economics textbook. But that doesn't mean that it fails to address the topic; on the contrary, God's Word has much to say about how we Christians should manage our money—or, more accurately, the money that God has *allowed* us to manage.

Living Outside of Normal Economics

God has told His followers this:

Let your conversation [manner, way of living] be without covetousness; and be content with such things as ye have: for he hath said, I will never leave thee, nor forsake thee (Hebrews 13:5).

But my God shall supply all your need according to his riches in glory by Christ Jesus (Philippians 4:19).

"Therefore take no thought, saying, 'What shall we eat?' or, 'What shall we drink?' or, 'Wherewithal shall we be clothed?'...for your heavenly Father knoweth that ye have need of all these things. But seek ye first the kingdom of God, and his righteousness; and all these things shall be added unto you" (Jesus in Matthew 6:31-33).

Obviously this doesn't mean that Christians should just lie around all day waiting for God to provide. But the lives of Christians are often touched by God in ways unexplainable to the "laws" of economics. One of the most famous examples in the Bible of God's provision occurred when Jesus told Peter to pay his *"tribute"* (taxes) to the Roman government. To get the money, Jesus then told Peter this:

"[G]o thou to the sea, and cast an hook, and take up the fish that first cometh up; and when thou hast opened his mouth, thou shalt find a piece of money: that take, and give unto them" (Matthew 17:27).

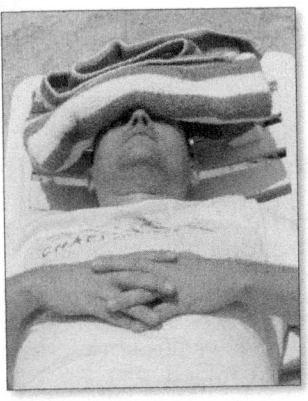

Just Waitin' on God to Provide

God has also worked miraculously in other ways, too: Deuteronomy 8 tells of how God kept the Hebrews' shoes and clothes from wearing out after their exodus from Egypt, even after they had been worn for 40 years.[3] And in 1 Kings 17, God kept the flour and oil of a widow from running out after she agreed to feed the prophet Elijah.

Closer to our modern day, God provided richly for George Müller (1805-1898), a Christian who famously directed an orphanage in England. Müller never once asked anyone for money, and he never took a salary. Instead, he simply prayed and trusted God to provide for his and the orphans' needs. One well-known incident happened like this:

"The children are dressed and ready for school. But there is no food for them to eat," the house-mother of the orphanage informed George Müller. George asked her to take the 300 children into the dining room and have them sit at the tables. He thanked God for the food and waited. George knew God would provide food for the children as he always did. Within minutes, a baker knocked on the door. "Mr. Müller," he said, "last night I could not sleep. Somehow I knew that you would need bread this morning. I got up and baked three batches for you. I will bring it in."

---

[3] They had probably gone out of style by then, however.

George Müller

Soon, there was another knock at the door. It was the milkman. His cart had broken down in front of the orphanage. The milk would spoil by the time the wheel was fixed. He asked George if he could use some free milk. George smiled as the milkman brought in ten large cans of milk. It was just enough for the 300 thirsty children."[4]

When I was 12, my family was in financial trouble, having moved a few months earlier to a new state. We had no money to pay the rent due. Just in time, however, a check came in the mail for the exact amount due (actually, a tiny bit more), from someone who had no idea that we needed money at all. Although this wasn't on the level of George Müller, it was a meaningful example of God's provision. Many Christians could tell similar stories!

Voluntary Giving and Blessing

In his brilliant 1850 essay *The Law*,[5] author Frederic Bastiat berates governments for plundering citizens and giving that plundered money to other citizens who didn't earn it. The word *plunder* is also translated *spoliation*, which is related to the word *spoil* (as in the saying "To the victor belong the spoils"—that is, a victorious army can steal everything from its defeated foes). Look at the form of the word *spoil* in the below passage, written by the Apostle Paul:

> For ye had compassion of me in my bonds, and took joyfully the spoiling of your goods, knowing in yourselves that ye have in heaven a better and an enduring substance (Hebrews 10:34).

Here Paul says to a group of his fellow Christians that they supported him by "*the spoiling of [their] goods,*" meaning that they gave up their property and money to provide for the needs of Paul, and no doubt others. The way Paul writes makes it sound as if those Christians were robbed, but, of course, they gave to Paul and to other Christians willingly! And look what else God's Word says about providing for others:

> When thou cuttest down thine harvest in thy field, and hast forgot a sheaf in the field, thou shalt not go again to fetch it: it shall be for the stranger, for the fatherless, and for the widow: that the LORD thy God may bless thee in all the work of thine hands. When thou beatest thine olive tree, thou shalt not go over the boughs again: it shall be for the stranger, for the fatherless, and for the widow. When thou gatherest the grapes of thy vineyard, thou shalt not glean it afterward: it shall be for the stranger, for the fatherless, and for the widow (Deuteronomy 24:19-21).

---

[4] "A Famous Story About George Müller's Faith," June 29, 2016, georgemuller.org/devotional/a-famous-story-about-mullers-faith.
[5] My one-semester civics course uses a book titled *Civics for Christian Homeschoolers*, which includes *The Law*; more information may be found at the front of this book.

But this I say, "He which soweth sparingly shall reap also sparingly; and he which soweth bountifully shall reap also bountifully. Every man according as he purposeth in his heart, so let him give; not grudgingly, or of necessity: for God loveth a cheerful giver" (2 Corinthians 9:6-7).

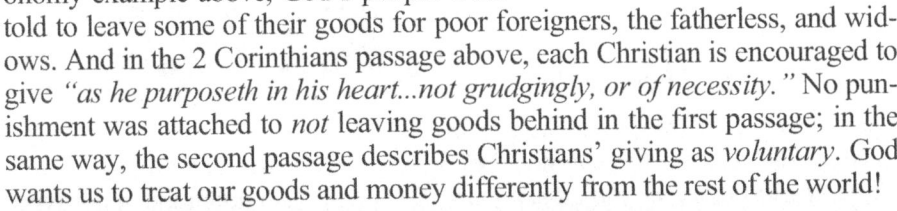

When God's people give, sometimes He uses their gifts to work *outside* of the normal, observable economy, turning their giving into a harvest of both spiritual riches and earthly provision that often can't be explained with a calculator. In the Deuteronomy example above, God's people were told to leave some of their goods for poor foreigners, the fatherless, and widows. And in the 2 Corinthians passage above, each Christian is encouraged to give *"as he purposeth in his heart...not grudgingly, or of necessity."* No punishment was attached to *not* leaving goods behind in the first passage; in the same way, the second passage describes Christians' giving as *voluntary*. God wants us to treat our goods and money differently from the rest of the world!

What Do You Think?

1. Can you think of another example in the Bible in which God made a supernatural provision for someone?
2. Can you remember a time that God miraculously provided for you or your family? What happened? Now, take time to thank Him!
3. Fill in the blanks to finish this passage: "Every man according as he purposeth in his heart, so let him ___; not ___, or of ___, for God loveth ___" (2 Corinthians 9:6-7).

1.3 – Should the Government Interfere in the Economy?

"What's the Best Way for Government to Control the Economy?"

For most of history, *economics* has, unfortunately, been tied up with government actions. Many powerful dictators have taken over buying and selling decisions of individuals as a means of exercising control over them. But many other rulers and lawmakers have also actually believed—based on their status as authorities—that they had the ability and the right to try to control the economies of "their" nations instead of simply leaving individuals alone to buy and sell how they thought best. Even today, many authorities and other leaders (government officials, college professors, etc.) casually discuss how they believe their government ought to, for example, "encourage" the pickled beet industry, or how much of a tariff (tax) the government should add to imported steel, or what license should be required for someone who wants to sell pizzas or cut hair or fix cars. But rarely do these supposed experts consider this: *Maybe the government doesn't **need** to "encourage" industries, or protect them from foreign competitors, or require a license for sellers of goods and services before they're allowed to operate.*

And *why* doesn't that quite reasonable idea occur to them? Partly because they don't know—or they don't care—what the *Bible* says are the true purposes of government.

Terror, Evil, and Economics

One of the most important disagreements economists have—if not *the* most important—is *to what extent a government should intervene in a nation's economy.* We'll talk later about the major types of economies. But first, if we're going to approach economics from a Biblical viewpoint, we've got to nail down the answer to this question: *What does God's Word say are government's true, moral purposes?* These:

1. **Government is to threaten and punish violence and theft.**
2. **Government is to provide justice.**

These four verses, two from the Old Testament, two from the New Testament, sum up the Bible's consistent message to rulers: how they are to fulfill government's legitimate purposes:

- *Thus saith the Lord GOD; "Let it suffice you, O princes of Israel: remove violence and spoil, and execute judgment and justice" (Ezekiel 45:9).*

- *Thus saith the LORD [to kings/rulers]; "Execute ye judgment and righteousness, and deliver the spoiled out of the hand of the oppressor: and do no wrong, do no violence to the stranger, the fatherless, nor the widow, neither shed innocent blood in this place" (Jeremiah 22:3).*

- *For rulers are not a terror to good works, but to the evil....for he [the ruler] is the minister of God, a revenger to execute wrath upon him that doeth evil (Romans 13:3-4).*

- *Submit yourselves to every ordinance of man for the Lord's sake: whether it be to the king, as supreme; or unto governors, as unto them that are sent by him for the punishment of evildoers (1 Peter 2:13-14).*

The word **evil** in the third passage, and the word **evildoers** in the last passage, are used in the Bible to refer to actions that wrongly **harm** others' persons (bodies) and property, not to actions that are simply *sinful*—like hatred or drunkenness or adultery—that do not harm others in the same way.

The above verses teach this: (1) The moral, legitimate purpose of government is to punish those who steal from others (*"spoil"*), or those who kill, injure, assault, kidnap, or otherwise wrongly **harm** others; (2) rulers ought to judge cases fairly and justly, and they have no business committing violence against their subjects, especially the weak and the vulnerable; and (3) the government's punishments of violent and thieving persons ought to strike fear into others tempted to commit similar crimes.

• • • • •

The above four verses don't represent an exhaustive list of everything that the Bible says about government; hundreds of other verses exist. But the Bible's consistent message in those many other verses can be boiled down to what is said in the above four.

And by the way, here's a beautiful verse that contrasts what the Bible says that governments ought to deter and punish:

> *And he made his grave with the wicked, and with the rich in his death; because he had done no violence, neither was any deceit in his mouth (Isaiah 53:9).*

Of course, the prophet Isaiah wrote this about the Lord Jesus Christ roughly 700 years before He was born on earth. What kind of a man and savior was Jesus on earth? That verse says that He was buried surrounded by sinners, and in a rich man's tomb, but He committed no wrong *violence* against anyone— exactly what God's Word says that governments are supposed to punish. And Jesus had no *deceit in his mouth*. In other words, He never told a lie. He also never committed fraud against or stole from anyone, which are matters that God's Word says in those four representative verses on the previous page that governments are to come down against.

> **The Bible says the reason governments exist is to threaten and punish violent evildoers and thieves.**

• • • • •

You will find no command of God saying that rulers of the world are to direct the economies of "their" nations. But does that mean government officials should *never* concern themselves with business or trade?

Of course not!

If a business, through its operations, kills or injures someone, or steals from or defrauds someone, that's when a government ought to step in. The same is true if a business damages or destroys someone's property. In those cases, government should *"execute judgment and justice"* by charging that business owner with a crime (if that violation was done on purpose, of course), finding him guilty in court (assuming he's guilty, of course), and ordering him to pay restitution to his victim, along with any other appropriate punishment.

Avoiding Two Giant Mistakes

*The reasons that governments are put on earth, according to the Bible, are **extremely** limited. Be sure you grasp this extremely important concept!*

This limited scope is completely sensible and just, when we stop to think about it, even in our modern society (no surprise there; the Bible has been miles ahead of everyone else on many topics for thousands of years). But sometimes it's hard to keep our focus on the *true, moral* purpose of government. That's especially true today, when it seems like so many today want the government to provide them with freebies—health care, education, a job, pork chops, back scratches, etc. So make sure you *really* commit those four short passages to memory; they make it very easy in most cases to determine whether a government policy or law is just.

We can see that God did not put governments in charge of "running the economy" at all. Instead, He carefully limited their legitimate purposes. If a government were limited to addressing these areas only, that would mean that it would be prohibited from meddling in the economy, *unless* it meant executing justice against a business that harmed or defrauded a customer or employee. A nation with that kind of government would benefit economically in many ways, including these two key ones:

1. Rulers at all government levels would not be tempted to pass trade laws that enriched themselves or their friends or their voters...by stealing from everybody else.
2. Rulers would be unable to pass a law to "fix an economic problem" that they see, which might superficially "fix" the problem, but harm the economy in other ways those rulers never thought of.

Many government officials (and economists) fall for that second temptation. They see Problem A in a nation's economy, and they propose a solution that focus-es on the group *directly* affected by Problem A. But those government officials and economists fail to see how their new government economic policy might affect *other* groups in that nation's economy *besides* the one they're trying to help get through Problem A.

In his classic 1946 book *Economics in One Lesson*, author Henry Hazlitt points out that bad economists often make two main mistakes. First, they look at a new economic policy's effects on only *a single* group (like the rulers in #2 above trying to help the Problem A group). Second, bad economists look at a new economic policy's effects only in the *short* term, not the long term. As Hazlitt puts it:

Henry Hazlitt

The art of economics consists in looking not merely at the immediate, but at the longer effects of any act or policy; it consists in tracing the consequences of that policy not merely for one group, but for all groups.[6]

A Sensible Ruler's Response

To finish this section, think about a rational, scrupulous person placed into a position of governmental authority. If someone were to try to talk that person into approving a proposed law that interfered in buying or selling or some other aspect of the economy, what would that sensible, honest person think? Probably something like this:

> *I'd better not push this proposed economic policy upon our nation, since I'm not sure of all the consequences it might create down the road. The new policy might appear to help the group that these government officials claim that they want to help, but...who knows? It might hurt **other** groups. And since I'm not a genius who's able to predict what millions of individuals will do—and neither are the lawmakers who sent me this bill to sign, come to think of it—I have no moral right to impose this law upon everybody.*
>
> *And as long as I'm being rational and sensible, I have to also say that I have no idea why people wear baseball caps backwards.*

What Do You Think?

1. Sum up what the Bible says are the legitimate functions of government.
2. Fill in these blanks: The Bible says that rulers are to "remove ___ and ___, and execute ___ and ___" (Ezekiel 45:9), and "deliver the ___ out of the hand of the ___" (Jeremiah 22:3). "For rulers are not a ___ to good works, but to the ___" (Romans 13:3-4), and they are "sent by him for the ___ of ___" (1 Peter 2:14).
3. What two major mistakes does Henry Hazlitt say bad economists make?
4. Fill in the blanks to finish these passages: "The fear of the LORD is the ___: a good ___ have all they that do his commandments" (Psalm 111:10); "I understand more than the ancients, because I ___" (Psalm 119:100).
5. ~~Why on earth do people wear baseball caps backwards anyway? Don't they know the whole point of the cap's bill is to keep the sun out of their eyes?~~

1.4 – CLAIM: "You Should <u>Have</u> to Give to the Poor!" • Quiz 1

After a college economics class you're taking, students are milling around, discussing what was said that day. You overhear one student saying this to another:

---

[6] Henry Hazlitt, *Economics In One Lesson* (Ludwig von Mises Institute, 2008), 5.

You Christians *don't* care about the poor, *or* even follow the Bible! God told the Hebrews in Leviticus 23:22 *not* to glean every corner of their fields, so the poor could have what was left over. If you were *really* a Christian, you'd sup-port a law that *made* all working Americans give part of their income to the poor.

How could you respond to this claim, using what you've learned? Jot down ideas (and if you're in my online or in-person class, bring them to class AND take Quiz 1; see below!).

 Take Quiz 1 (online or in-person students only). Feel free to use your notes, but there is a time limit!

2.1 – How To Use Man's Selfishness for Economic Good

How Mankind Acts: No Mystery At All

In case you had any doubts on whether mankind in general is selfish and sinful, just watch the news tonight, or take a look around you when you're with a crowd.[7] Humans habitually put themselves before others, and that's something that God's Word points out many times. For example:

- *"Thou shalt love thy neighbor as thyself" (Matthew 22:39).*
- *Look not every man on his own things, but every man also on the things of others (Philippians 2:4).*
- *Let no man seek his own, but every man another's wealth (1 Corinthians 10:24).*
- *For no man ever yet hated his own flesh; but nourisheth and cherisheth it, even as the Lord the church (Ephesians 5:29).*

In the first verse, Jesus said His followers should love their neighbors as much as they love themselves—which, of course, assumes that they love themselves a great deal.

The second and third verses command Christians not just to care about their *own* needs, but others' needs (same assumption as the first verse).

The last verse says that members of the human race do not hate themselves, but tend to put their own needs first. No surprise there!

Perceptive individuals who are not necessarily Christian also confirm this characteristic of mankind. In his famous 1850 political essay *The Law*, French author Frederic Bastiat notes that mankind has a "fatal tendency": the desire to have his needs met *without having to endure the struggle of working* to meet those needs. This desire also demonstrates man's strong inclination to take care

---

[7] Be sure not to make eye contact.

> The Bible, history, and experience assure us that man acts in his own self-interest.

of his *own* needs first. Author and salesman Harry Browne makes a similar point about man's nature, as he advises those in the field of sales to think about the typical person to whom they are trying to sell a product or service:

> ...[L]et's analyze the typical prospect you meet in your selling day. What do we know about him?
>
> We know that he's seeking the best possible life for himself. His resources are limited, however; he has only so much time and energy and money. So he must allocate those resources on some basis that will bring him as much as possible.
>
> He makes plans and programs, ways of getting what he wants. His motivations are the goals at the end of those plans. He knows what it is he wants, and he has some idea of how to get it.[8]

How Mankind's Tendency Can Guide Economics

Imagine you are the newly elected ruler of a nation. You have no idea about the legitimate purposes of government that the Bible lays out, but you are determined to rule justly. If you were given the power to influence what kind of economic system "your" nation pursues, what would you do about the tendency of human beings to pursue their own interests first? Would you pursue a policy that...

1. acknowledges that humans are basically self-seeking and generally first look out for their own interests, or
2. ignores this universal human tendency and forces individuals in various ways to give part of their property or money to others who didn't earn it?

We'll dive into that topic soon, but be aware that the two above choices represent drastically different economic philosophies. The first is often called *capitalism* or *voluntary exchange*, and the second *socialism* or *communism*. But regardless of their names, clearly the more sensible, rational—and Biblical!—choice is the first one. One economic writer who famously ad-dressed this topic was Scotsman Adam Smith (1723-1790). In 1776 Smith wrote a highly influential work called *An Inquiry into the Nature and Causes of the Wealth of Nations*, usually just called *The Wealth of Nations*. One of the most well-known passages from that work reads this way:

Adam Smith

---

[8] Harry Browne, *The Secret of Selling Anything* (Harry Browne, 2008), 56.

It is not from the benevolence of the butcher, the brewer, or the baker that we expect our dinner, but from their regard to their own self-interest. We address ourselves, not to their humanity, but to their self-love, and never talk to them of our own necessities but of their advantages. Nobody but a beggar chooses to depend chiefly upon the benevolence of his fellow-citizens. Even a beggar does not depend upon it entirely. The charity of well-disposed people, indeed, supplies him with the whole fund of his subsistence. But though this principle ultimately provides him with all the necessaries of life which he has occasion for, it neither does nor can provide him with them as he has occasion for them. The greater part of his occasional wants are supplied in the same manner as those of other people: by treaty, by barter, and by purchase. With the money which one man gives him he purchases food. The old clothes which another bestows upon him he exchanges for other old clothes which suit him better, or for lodging, or for food, or for money, with which he can buy either food, clothes, or lodging, as he has occasion.[9]

> **In other words, a free-trade (voluntary-exchange) economy does *not* work because producers of goods and services and labor are *first* generously and unselfishly looking out for *others*. It works because those producers are first looking out for *themselves*—just like we would expect from what the Bible teaches and what we see in the real world every day.**

How do those who participate in a voluntarily cooperating economy ensure that they have money to buy critically important items like food, clothing, housing, medical care, and rainbow-colored toe socks? *By producing things like labor or goods or services that please **others** in that same economy—others who are happy to pay for them.*

In this free-trade "system," no one is forced to work to benefit *others*... but benefiting others is exactly what ends up happening anyway! Just like Harry Browne pointed out on the previous page, and Adam Smith pointed out in *The Wealth of Nations*, all those who buy from or sell to others do so **because they expect to benefit themselves.**

What Do You Think?

1. What does the command of Jesus to "love thy neighbor as thyself" reveal about man's natural tendency? Besides the examples given in this chapter, list one more that confirms this tendency.
2. Explain Adam Smith's main point in the passage near this chapter's end.
3. Fill in the blanks to finish these passages: "Look not every man on his ___, but every man also on the ___" (Philippians 2:4); "Let no man seek ___, but every

---

[9] "Adam Smith on the Butcher, the Brewer, and the Baker," Online Library of Liberty, https://oll.libertyfund.org/quote/adam-smith-butcher-brewer-baker.

man another's ___" (1 Corinthians 10:24); "For no man ever hated ___; but nourisheth it and cherisheth it..." (Ephesians 5:29).

2.2 – "The True Functions of Government"

William Leggett (1801-1839) was an American author and defender of economic freedom. He wrote the following article, first published on November 21, 1834, in the *New York Evening Post*, a daily newspaper (now the *New York Post*) that is still going strong. The *Post's* editor, August Glen-James, wrote this introduction, which was published along with the article:

William Leggett

> What the "true functions of government" should be are of interest to all involved in any kind of body politic. Of course, opinions differ. Some positions are rooted in a collectivist assumption about society; others from an individualist assumption. To all, however, Leggett's thoughts should be interesting and thought provoking.

• • • • •

The True Functions of Government

There are no necessary evils in government. Its evils exist only in its abuses. If it would confine itself to *equal protection*, and, as heaven does its rains, shower its favors alike on the high and the low, the rich and the poor, it would be an unqualified blessing.

This is the language of our venerated [respected] President,[10] and the passage deserves to be written in letters of gold, for neither in truth of sentiment or beauty of expression can it be surpassed. We choose it as our text for a few remarks on the true functions of Government.

The fundamental principle of all governments is the protection of person and property from domestic and foreign enemies; in other words, to defend the weak against the strong. By establishing the social feeling in a community, it was intended to counteract that selfish feeling, which, in its proper exercise, is the parent of all worldly good, and, in its excesses, the root of all evil. The functions of Government, when confined to their proper sphere of action, are therefore restricted to the making of *general laws*, uniform and universal in their operation, for these purposes, and for no other.

Governments have no right to interfere with the pursuits of individuals, as guaranteed by those general laws, by offering encouragements and granting privileges to any particular class of industry, or any select bodies of men, inas-

---

[10] At the time the President was Andrew Jackson.

much as all classes of industry and all men are equally important to the general welfare, and equally entitled to protection.

Whenever a Government assumes the power of discriminating between the different classes of the community, it becomes, in effect, the arbiter [judge] of their prosperity, and exercises a power not contemplated by any intelligent people in delegating their sovereignty to their rulers. It then becomes the great regulator of the profits of every species of industry, and reduces men from a dependence on their own exertions [labors], to a dependence on the caprices [whims, arbitrary or biased decisions] of their Government. Governments possess no delegated right to tamper with individual industry a single hair's breadth beyond what is essential to protect the rights of person and property.

• • • • •

In the exercise of this power of intermeddling with the private pursuits and individual occupations of the citizen, a Government may...elevate one class and depress another; it may one day legislate exclusively for the farmer, the next for the mechanic, and the third for the manufacturer, who all thus become the mere puppets of legislative cobbling and tinkering, instead of independent citizens, relying on their own resources for their prosperity. It assumes the functions which belong alone to an overruling Providence [God], and affects to become the universal dispenser of good and evil.

This power of regulating—of increasing or diminishing the profits of labor and the value of property of all kinds and degrees, by direct legislation.... destroys the essential object of all civil compacts [agreements], which, as we said before, is to make the social a counterpoise [balance] to the selfish feeling. By thus operating directly on the latter, by offering one class a bounty and another a discouragement, they involve the selfish feeling in every struggle of party for the ascendancy [dominance], and give to the force of political rivalry all the bitterest excitement of personal interests conflicting with each other. Why is it that parties now exhibit excitement aggravated to a degree dangerous to the existence of the Union and to the peace of society? Is it not that by frequent exercises of partial legislation, almost every man's personal interests have become deeply involved in the result of the contest? In common times, the strife of parties is the mere struggle of ambitious leaders for power; now they are deadly contests of the whole mass of the people, whose pecuniary [financial] interests are implicated in the event, because the Government has usurped and exercised the power of legislating on their private affairs. The selfish feeling has been so strongly called into action by this abuse of authority as almost to overpower the social feeling, which it should be the object of a good Government to foster by every means in its power.

No nation, knowingly and voluntarily...ever delegated to its Government this enormous power, which places at its disposal the property, the industry, and the fruits of the industry, of the whole people. As a general rule, the prosperity of rational men depends on themselves. Their talents and their virtues shape their fortunes. They are therefore the best judges of their own affairs and should be permitted to seek their own happiness in their own way, untrammeled [unrestrained] by the capricious [impulsive] interference of legislative bungling, so long as they do not violate the equal rights of others, nor transgress...laws for the security of person and property.

· · · · ·

But modern refinements have introduced new principles in the science of Government. Our own Government, most especially, has assumed and exercised an authority over the people, not unlike that of weak and vacillating [indecisive] parents over their children, and with about the same degree of impartiality [fairness]. One child becomes a favorite because he has made a fortune, and another because he has failed in the pursuit of that object; one because of its beauty, and another because of its deformity. Our Government has thus exercised the right of dispensing favors to one or another class of citizens at will; of directing its patronage [support] first here and then there; of bestowing one day and taking back the next; of giving to the few and denying to the many; of investing wealth with new and exclusive privileges, and distributing, as it were at random, and with a capricious policy, in unequal portions, what it ought not to bestow, or what, if given away, should be equally the portion of all.

A government administered on such a system of policy may be called a Government of Equal Rights, but it is in its nature and essence a disguised despotism [tyranny]. It is the capricious dispenser of good and evil, without any restraint, except its own sovereign will. It holds in its hand the distribution of the goods of this world, and is consequently the uncontrolled master of the people.

Such was not the object of the Government of the United States, nor such the powers delegated to it by the people. The object was beyond doubt to protect the weak against the strong, by giving them an equal voice and equal rights in the state; not to make one portion stronger, the other weaker at pleasure, by crippling one or more classes of the community, or making them tributary [inferior] to one alone. This is too great a power to entrust to Government. It was never given away by the people, and is not a right, but a usurpation [violation].

Experience will show that this power has always been exercised under the influence and for the exclusive benefit of wealth. It was never wielded on behalf of the community. Whenever an exception is made to the general law of the land, founded on the principle of equal rights, it will always be found to be in favor of wealth. These immunities are never bestowed on the poor. They have no claim to a dispensation [giving out] of exclusive benefit, and their only business is to *"take care of the rich that the rich may take care of the poor."*

Thus it will be seen that the sole reliance of the laboring classes, who constitute a vast majority of every people on the earth, is the great principle of Equal Rights; that their only safeguard against oppression is a system of legislation which leaves all to the free exercise of their talents and industry, within the limits of the GENERAL LAW, and which, on no pretense of public good, bestows on any particular class of industry, or any particular body of men, rights or privileges not equally enjoyed by the great aggregate [total, whole] of the body politic....

What Do You Think?

Explain in your own words what Leggett means by the following statements in the above essay, and how they agree with what God's Word says about economics:

- "Governments possess no...right to tamper with individual industry...beyond what is essential to protect the rights of person and property."
- "By offering one class a bounty and another a discouragement, they involve the selfish feeling in every struggle of party for the ascendancy, and give to the force of political rivalry all the bitterest excitement of personal interests conflicting with each other."
- "[The people] are...the best judges of their own affairs, and should be permitted to seek their own happiness in their own way, untrammeled by the...interference of legislative bungling, so long as they do not violate the equal rights of others, nor transgress the general laws for the security of person and property."

Fill in the blanks to finish these passages:

- "The fear ___ is the beginning of ___" (Psalm 111:10).
- "Every man according as he purposeth in his ___, so let him ___; not ___, or of ___: for God loveth ___" (2 Corinthians 9:6-7).

2.3 – Camels, Needles, Moths, and Eagles

Christians, Work, and Riches

When God placed man in the Garden of Eden, He gave him *work* to do. Work is still today a necessary and fulfilling part of life, but humans can still take it to extremes. A few examples:

- Some do all they can to *avoid* work.
- Some are "workaholics" who want to do nothing but work all the time.
- Some work for the sole purpose of accumulating wealth.

A person who works a great deal in a free country—or even a *somewhat* free country—can amass a considerable amount of wealth. A Christian perspective on work and earthly riches is enlightening and interesting; here are a few points that God's Word makes about those topics:

1. **Christians should work faithfully and do their best, so they'll honor—instead of shame—the name of Jesus.**

    - *For even when we were with you, this we commanded you, that if any would not work, neither should he eat. For we hear that there are some which walk among you disorderly, working not at all, but are busybodies. Now them that are such we command and exhort by our Lord Jesus Christ, that with quietness they work, and eat their own bread. (2 Thessalonians 3:10-12).*

    - *And...they* [young widows] *learn to be idle* [lazy, slothful], *wandering about from house to house; and not only idle, but tattlers also and busybodies, speaking things which they ought not (1 Timothy 5:13).*

    Comment: You don't want to work? Then you shouldn't eat. Even non-Christians instinctively know *that's* right. And those widows mentioned above didn't work or otherwise accomplish anything, so what happened? They were much more likely to waste their time, or worse, stir up trouble by gossiping.

2. **Christians are to work partly to support *others*, especially other needy Christians.**

    - *I have shewed you all things, how that so laboring ye ought to support the weak, and to remember the words of the Lord Jesus, how he said, "It is more blessed to give than to receive" (Acts 20:35).*

    - *That they* [the rich] *do good, that they be rich in good works, ready to distribute, willing to communicate* [give freely]; *laying up in store for themselves a good foundation against the time to come, that they may lay hold on eternal life (1 Timothy 6:18-19).*

    - *Hereby perceive we the love of God, because he laid down his life for us: and we ought to lay down our lives for the brethren. But whoso hath this world's good, and seeth his brother have need, and shutteth up his bowels of compassion from him, how dwelleth the love of God in him? My little children, let us not love in word, neither in tongue; but in deed and in truth (1 John 3:16-18).*

    - *Now concerning the collection for the saints, as I have given order to the churches...even so do ye. Upon the first day of the week let every one of you lay by him in store, as God hath prospered him, that there be no gatherings when I come (1 Corinthians 6:1-2).*

- *As every man hath received the gift, even so minister the same one to another, as good stewards[11] of the manifold grace of God (1 Peter 4:10).*

Comment: Jesus said, *"It is more blessed to give than to receive,"* one of the few things that we know He said outside the four gospels and the book of Revelation. Also, (a) rich Christians are to share with their needy brothers and sisters, (b) Christians who don't want to give to others can hardly call themselves Christians, and (c) Christians should set up some system as a body to provide for other Christians who have needs. In fact, this reporting on and giving to needy Christians—often to help the suffering widows and children of Christians who were jailed and killed for their faith—was a systematic part of the early church's meetings.

3. **Don't work just to be rich or pursue riches; they're temporary and won't bring ultimate happiness.**

    - *Labor not to be rich: cease from thine own wisdom. Wilt thou set thine eyes upon that which is not? For riches certainly make themselves wings; they fly away as an eagle toward heaven (Proverbs 23:4-5).*

    - *A faithful man shall abound with blessings: but he that maketh haste to be rich shall not be innocent (Proverbs 28:20).*

    - *He that loveth silver shall not be satisfied with silver; nor he that loveth abundance with increase: this is also vanity (Ecclesiastes 5:10).*

    - *And he [Jesus] said unto them, "Take heed, and beware of covetousness: for a man's life consisteth not in the abundance of the things which he possesseth" (Luke 12:15).*

    - *For we brought nothing into this world, and it is certain we can carry nothing out. And having food and raiment [clothes] let us be therewith content (1 Timothy 6:7-8).*

    - *Charge them that are rich in this world, that they be not highminded, nor trust in uncertain riches, but in the living God, who giveth us richly all things to enjoy (1 Timothy 6:17).*

    - *"Lay not up for yourselves treasures upon earth, where moth and rust doth corrupt, and where thieves break through and steal: but lay up for yourselves treasures in heaven, where neither moth nor rust doth corrupt, and where thieves do not break through nor steal:*

---

[11] There's that word again!

For where your treasure is, there will your heart be also" (Jesus in Matthew 6:19-21).

- *Let the brother of low degree rejoice in that he is exalted: but the rich, in that he is made low: because as the flower of the grass he shall pass away. For the sun is no sooner risen with a burning heat, but it withereth the grass, and the flower thereof falleth, and the grace of the fashion of it perisheth: so also shall the rich man fade away in his ways (James 1:9-11).*

Comment: How many people do you know who—without even knowing it—verify the accuracy of God's Word, which says that the rich are often unsatisfied? (Do you know anyone about your age who has a wealthy family, but is despondent a noticeable part of the time?) God also warns wealthy Christians not to be *"highminded"* or to *"trust in uncertain riches."* In fact, rich men are in some way seen as *"made low"* by God.

4. **The pursuit of riches can pull us away from God.**

    - *"No man can serve two masters: for either he will hate the one, and love the other; or else he will hold to the one, and despise the other. Ye cannot serve God and mammon [riches, wealth]" (Jesus in Matthew 6:24).*

    - *And Jesus looked round about, and saith unto his disciples, "How hardly shall they that have riches enter into the kingdom of God!" And the disciples were astonished at his words. But Jesus answereth again, and saith unto them, "Children, how hard is it for them that trust in riches to enter into the kingdom of God! It is easier for a camel to go through the eye of a needle, than for a rich man to enter into the kingdom of God" (Mark 10:23-25).*

    - *But they that will be rich fall into temptation and a snare, and into many foolish and hurtful lusts, which drown men in destruction and perdition. For the love of money is the root of all evil: which while some coveted after, they have erred from the faith, and pierced themselves through with many sorrows (1 Timothy 6:9).*

Comment: The rich—way back in the time of Jesus, and in our day—often think they've got it made on earth, so, unfortunately, they're more likely to give God short shrift. In contrast, God says that *"to this man will I look, even to him that is poor and of a contrite spirit, and trembleth at my word"* (Isaiah 66:2). The poor, back in the time of Jesus, and even today, are more apt to turn to God for help. And notice that Jesus doesn't say a man "will have a hard time serving two masters"; He says, *"No man **can** serve two masters."*

Finally, can you imagine the extra dangers and worries that an extremely wealthy person faces? (You can probably think of a few!)

Two Great "Riches Stories"

Let's finish with two great Christians and their beautiful testimonies on riches.

First, one from the English evangelist John Wesley (1703-1791). After once visiting a poor widow, Wesley realized that she was cold, since she had no warm coat. He reached into his pocket to give her some money to buy one, but realized that he had spent that money on a few pictures to decorate his home. Afterwards, Wesley he vowed to spend as little on himself as possible. In a sermon he later preached called "The Use of Money," he laid out three principles: (1) Gain all you can, (2), save all you can, and (3) give all you can.[12]

John Wesley

Second, J. Hudson Taylor (1832-1905), a British missionary to China, committed himself at a young age to live on as little as possible, so he could give more to others:

> I...found that I could live on very much less than I had previously thought possible. Butter, milk, and other luxuries I ceased to use, and found that by living mainly on oatmeal and rice, with occasional variations, a very small sum was sufficient for my needs. In this way, I had more than two-thirds of my income available for other purposes. And my experience was that the less I spent on myself, and the more I gave to others, the fuller of happiness and blessing did my soul become.[13]

J. Hudson Taylor

One more thing. When God was leading the Israelites toward the promised land, Moses pointed out that when they got there, God would bless them with many material things. Moses then warned the Israelites about a wrong attitude they might be tempted to have:

> "And thou say in thine heart, 'My power and the might of mine hand hath gotten me this wealth.' But thou shalt remember the LORD thy God: for it is he that giveth thee power to get wealth, that he may establish his covenant which he sware unto thy fathers, as it is this day" (Deuteronomy 8:17-18).

Do we work hard for money? Of course. (At least, those of us who have to work for money do.) Do we use our talents to produce wealth? Sure. But that

---

[12] Stephen Warren, "John Wesley's Three Rules for Use of Money," *Daily Press*, June 30, 2018, dailypress.com/life/dp-fea-religion-column-warren-0701-story.html.

[13] Dr. and Mrs. J. Hudson Taylor, *J. Hudson Taylor: God's Man in China* (Chicago Moody Press, 1965), 26.

doesn't mean we forget God, who has blessed us with inherent abilities. Everything we get in this life and the next is a blessing He allows us to have. And maybe the best testimony we could take to heart on the concept of riches is what Paul told the Corinthians about Jesus:

> *For ye know the grace of our Lord Jesus Christ, that, though he was rich, yet for your sakes he became poor, that ye through his poverty might be rich (2 Corinthians 8:9).*

What Do You Think?

1. Pretty much every Christian has heard many warnings about making the pursuit of riches his life's goal; it's a cliché, even among non-Christians. But what's a concrete way that we can make this a reality in our lives—maybe something that we're not doing now, but could change slightly, or even drastically, to honor what God's Word says about the topic?

2. Think up and write down at least one way that rich persons face troubles (how the rich have *"pierced themselves through with many sorrows"*)—troubles that the average person doesn't face. That is, do the rich worry about things that wealth has burdened them with more than others?

3. Fill in the blanks to finish these passages:
   - "The fear of the LORD is ___; a good __ have all they that do ___" (Psalm 111:10).
   - "A ___ giveth heed to false lips; and a ___ giveth ear to a naughty tongue" (Proverbs 17:4).
   - "Let no man seek ___; but every man another's ___" (1 Corinthians 10:24).
   - "For no man ever hated ___; but nourisheth and cherisheth it" (Ephesians 5:29).
   - "For we brought ___ into this world, and it is certain we can carry ___. And having ___ and ___ let us be therewith content" (1 Timothy 6:7-8).

2.4 – CLAIM: "We Have to Stop Those Robots!" • Quiz 2

Last week we heard from economics writer Henry Hazlitt, who pointed out that bad economists make two major mistakes. Do you recall what they are?

To refresh your memory, those mistakes are (a) looking at an economic policy's effects on only *one* group, instead of *all* groups; and (b) looking at an economic policy's effects only in the *short* run, and not in the *long* run.

One way that these two mistakes in economic thinking have manifested themselves has been how some individuals react to new machines, inventions, and technology. For hundreds of years, confused and/or misinformed persons have feared and protested the rise of industrial machines, as well as new technologies, since those machines and technological advancements have eliminated (or reduced) the need for certain jobs. Perhaps most famously, in the 1800s, a group of English stocking makers called **Luddites** protested the use of textile machines that put them out of work by destroying those machines and burning down the mills that used them.

But the types of machines and technologies that replace old ways of making products, offering services, and making modern life much safer and more convenient are too many to count. That doesn't mean, however, that modern-day Luddites aren't still out there.

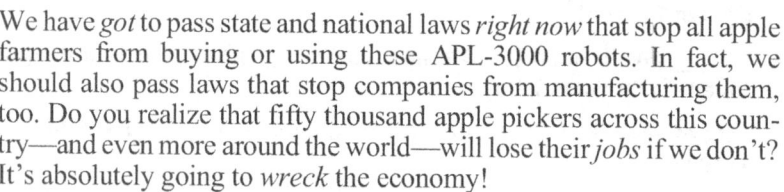

Let's say, for example, that someone invents a new apple harvesting robot, which we'll call the APL-3000. This machine greatly speeds up the gathering process for apple farmers. One evening, while watching the news on TV, you a reporter interviewing an angry apple picker representative. That representative tells the interviewer this:

> We have *got* to pass state and national laws *right now* that stop all apple farmers from buying or using these APL-3000 robots. In fact, we should also pass laws that stop companies from manufacturing them, too. Do you realize that fifty thousand apple pickers across this country—and even more around the world—will lose their *jobs* if we don't? It's absolutely going to *wreck* the economy!

Think for a minute of the effects on the economy that would result from the use of the APL-3000, then answer the questions below.

What Do You Think?

1. Write down two ways of doing things that nobody—or almost nobody—uses any more (producing goods and services, entertainment, transportation, medical care, and so on—any good examples you can think of).
2. Take one example you thought of from #1 and write down the more modern or efficient method or technology that has <u>replaced</u> the old method.
3. In your favorite example, what groups lost their jobs when the old method was replaced?
4. What various jobs were <u>created</u> by the new technology?
5. In the APL-3000 example, how do you think the robots affected in the long term (a) the number of apples farmers could harvest in one season, and (b) the cost of apples to consumers? →

6. Would the widespread use of the APL-3000 be an overall benefit or detriment to society? Why?
7. How is opposing machinery that performs jobs—even if that machinery replaces workers—a perfect example of Henry Hazlitt's definition of the two main types of bad economic thinking?
8. How would a government's interfering in the development and use of machinery violate the Bible's standards? What would be crazy about the government's even trying to do it anyway?

Take Quiz 2 (online or in-person students only).
Feel free to use your notes, but there is a time limit!

3.1 – The Right to Property

No Private Property?

In November 2016, the World Economic Forum (WEF), a dangerous organization that favors a one-world government, tweeted a message that expressed its vision of the future for everyone, starting in 2030: "You'll own nothing, and you'll be happy."

Of course, questions come to the minds of many after reading this message. The first might be this: Did the WEF mean to say in that tweet that its members, bankers, politicians, kings, presidents, and all millionaires and billionaires will also eagerly join the rest of the world on the "own nothing" trend?

The second might be this: How, exactly, does the WEF plan to arrange it so everyone owns nothing? If there's a new car sitting on the road, whose is it? Can I just jump in the driver's seat and take off in it if I want to, as long as no one else is using it (or at least, no one else stronger than I am is using it)? And can I just drive up to any grocery store I come across and help myself to a few cans of pickled beets and a handful of rib-eye steaks? And if there's not enough gas in that car to get to the grocery store, can I just fill it up for free, and drive off without paying, with a honk and a little wave?

And what about those who still *want* to own things?

Of course, the WEF's goal for everyone on earth to "own nothing" really doesn't mean it wants to make everyone jolly and carefree by not having to worry about owning anything. Notice that the tweet did *not* say this:

"*We'll* own nothing, and *we'll* be happy."

What the WEF *really* meant was this: "*We* and our cronies will own everything, including you." Because expecting no one to own anything is a completely crackpot idea. It violates the personal experience and God-given instincts of every person on earth who hasn't been repeatedly kicked in the head by a mule. And you won't be surprised to learn that it totally contradicts the Bible's teachings, which consistently recognize and uphold the concept of private property.

The Bible and Private Property

God's Word clearly upholds the concept of private property, as demonstrated in these and many other verses:

- Bible verses like *"Thou shalt not steal"* (Exodus 20:15), *"Thou shalt not covet"* (Exodus 20:17), and *"Let him that stole steal no more"* (Ephesians 4:28) only make sense if somebody *owns* that property that is wrongly being stolen or coveted.

- After Ananias and Sapphira pretended to give their local church all the money they made from selling their property, Peter said to them, *"Whiles it remained, was it not thine own?"* (Acts 5:4), since he knew that it was previously *their* property!

- In the parable of the man who hired laborers to work in his fields (although the man represented God), Jesus indirectly affirmed the right of employers to do what they wanted to with their own property or money (Matthew 20:1-15).

We've seen that the Bible says that government's *moral, true* purpose is to protect against and punish violations against persons and their property—assault, kidnapping, murder, rape, theft, and so on. This view supports the idea that, humanly speaking, a person "owns himself."[14] Frederic Bastiat, in *The Law*, also affirms this basic principle:

> ...[P]ersonality, liberty, property—this is man. And regardless of what dishonest politicians say, these three things came *before* man-made laws and are superior to them. It is not because men have made laws, that personality, liberty, and property exist. On the contrary, it is because personality, liberty, and property exist *before-*

---

[14] Of course, Christians see this differently, because as the Bible says to us in 1 Corinthians 7:23, *"Ye are bought with a price."*

hand that men make laws....All the law's actions should be in favor of protecting property, and against stealing property.

Christians' view of their property will add key elements, including acknowledgements that (1) God owns everything; (2) we should be willing to give up our property for the good of others, especially needy Christians; and (3) those who give to others will be blessed by doing so:

> *"For every beast of the forest is mine, and the cattle upon a thousand hills. I know all the fowls of the mountains: and the wild beasts of the field are mine" (God in Psalm 50:10-11).*
>
> *The earth is the LORD's, and the fulness thereof; the world, and they that dwell therein (Psalm 24:1).*
>
> *The liberal [freely giving, blessing] soul shall be made fat: and he that watereth shall be watered also himself (Proverbs 11:25).*
>
> *He that giveth unto the poor shall not lack: but he that hideth his eyes shall have many a curse (Proverbs 28:27).*
>
> *As we have therefore opportunity, let us do good unto all men, especially unto them who are of the household of faith (Galatians 6:10).*

> **The law's purpose is to protect against and punish violations against persons and their property.**

• • • • •

Private property is necessary (a) for an economy to grow, (b) to foster work and trade, and (c) to satisfy the productive, healthful inner urge of mankind to accomplish things and be rewarded for working. In a free economy, *the rewards earned* by those who produce goods and services that please others—cars, babysitting, apples, mobile phones, a repaired broken bone, a pair of eyeglasses, math tutoring, chicken sandwiches with two little pickles on them (with waffle fries), and so on—are the reason we have so much readily available food, clothing, and technology today.

> **Private property rights are clearly and consistently supported in God's Word, which means that they are sensible and just. They are an important component of law and civilization.**

What Do You Think?

1. Give proof that God's Word upholds private property. Can you think of any more examples from the Bible that affirm this right? →

2. **Explain what you think would happen if there were no private property. For example, what if no one owned the food in your local grocery store, or if everybody owned it equally?**
3. **Answer the questions in the third paragraph in this section about the WEF's desire for a world in which no one owns anything.**

3.2 – Economics Terms You Should Know

Most studies of economics include many terms—not as complicated as the one we thought about teaching to that group of toddlers a few chapters back, but more manageable. And although it's better to have an overall understanding of real-life economics, instead of slavishly focusing on memorizing terms, here are several economics terms it's helpful to know:

Scarcity and Opportunity Cost

Scarcity refers to the rarity of something, like water in a desert, or excitement when watching golf on TV. In economics it means that consumers—even the very richest ones—can't have everything they want, because materials on earth used to create those goods and services consumers want are limited.[15] Since consumers can't have everything they want, they must make choices. You have done this countless times in your life, no doubt. Let's say that you have an hour to spend before you have to go to work. You can either (a) take a nap, or (b) study for a quiz—but not both. Likewise, you might have some money and realize that you can either (a) buy a pair of sandals, or (b) buy essential oil as an emollient for your burst appendix.

An **opportunity cost** is what a person gives up in pursuit of something else. In the first example above, if you decided to spend the hour studying for your quiz, your opportunity cost would be the rest you could have had from the nap. And if you decided to take a nap, your opportunity cost would be the higher score you could have received on the quiz. In the second example, if you decided to buy the sandals, the opportunity cost would be the better feeling in your appendix area. If you decided to buy the essential oil, your opportunity cost would be the sandals.

Micro and Macro, Austrian and Keynesian

The English prefix "micro" comes from a Greek word meaning "small" and is used in words like *microwave, microscope, microchip,* and *microphone.* Likewise, the study of **microeconomics** focuses more on "small," *individual* economic choices. The prefix "macro" comes from a Greek word meaning

---

[15] We also all have a scarcity of *time*, both in the long run and short run. That is, we only have so many hours a day to work or pursue our goals, so we must manage our time, and we have on-ly a certain number of years to live to do the same thing.

"long" and is used as a prefix in words like *macrobiotics*. The term **macroeconomics** refers to the study of larger-scale *collective* economic behaviors in an entire city, state, or nation.

Authorities and economists who favor government meddling in economies often focus on macroeconomics. They hold the strange belief that they can fix a nation's economic problems with policies *forced* upon the people—policies they think will push the public into making "correct" decisions.[16] Those with this view often call themselves **Keynesians**, after English economist John Maynard Keynes (1883-1946), an advocate of government interference in economies. Keynesians often try "fixing" economies by arranging for the government to...

John Maynard Keynes

1. tax imported goods so consumers "buy local," instead of buying similar, cheaper foreign goods;
2. control how much of a good is produced;
3. set prices for goods and services;
4. spend government (taxpayer) funds on jobs or other programs that are supposed to "stimulate" the economy; and
5. print new money and hand it out to the people—again, supposedly to "stimulate" the economy.

Ludwig von Mises

Other economists believe that governments should stay out of the economy—unless fraud or violence has been committed, of course—and that individuals should be free to make their own economic decisions, more at the "microeconomic" level. These economists are sometimes called **Austrian** economists, after the champion of free-market economics Ludwig von Mises (1881-1973), who was from Austria. Austrian economists logically insist that every economy is made up of *individuals* who make billions of decisions every day that can't be predicted by government planners. Why? Because (a) no group of government planners on earth can predict what millions of buyers and sellers will do, and (b) buyers and consumers sometimes make choices that seem irrational. That is, their economic choices, which are presumably made based on scarcity and taking into account the opportunity costs like the ones we reviewed on the previous page—can't be predicted with anywhere close to 100 percent accuracy.

In other words, everybody's different! For example, which is the better choice: a drab gray coat that keeps the wearer warm in the freezing cold, or a

---

[16] It rarely seems to occur to these planners that they might be wrong, however.

stylish yellow coat that doesn't keep the wearer as warm? No doubt the gray coat, but who knows what some coat buyers will choose? It might be that they're willing to put up with their opportunity cost of being cold to look fashionable, even though a government planner might say, "They shouldn't do *that*! The *correct* choice is the gray coat; it's warmer!" Now, if the winter is bitterly cold, and consumers realize the worth of the gray coat versus the snazzier yellow coat, no doubt most will buy gray coats (if those are the only two choices, of course). But should government officials have the right—as well as the *power*—to direct consumers into what kind of coat—or any other product—they must buy?

You won't be surprised to learn that Austrian economists say that such meddlers are wildly overstepping their proper boundaries—and ridiculously arrogant to boot—when they try to order sellers what items to produce and how much to charge for them. Government economic planners and big-government-favoring economists are famous for making the two main mistakes that we saw Henry Hazlitt point out in a previous chapter.

(Do you remember what those two mistakes were?)

And sometimes, because consumers have different opinions and values, they just flat-out make seemingly "wrong" choices when they buy and sell goods and services, and then they must face the consequences of those poor decisions. But remember what the Bible, all human history, and your own experience reveal about how men and women act in their own self-interest?[17] This happens across an economy individually, which affects the entire economy. Austrian economist Roger Garrison (1944—) coined a beautifully short and sweet adage to describe this phenomenon:

> There are macroeconomic problems, but only microeconomic solutions.[18]

Do you understand what Garrison is saying? He's pointing out that leaving individuals alone to make their own decisions *works*, not government meddling to try to force everyone to do this or that. Garrison, by the way, is a *macroeconomist*. (Just because someone is an Austrian economist doesn't mean he only studies microeconomics; just because someone is a Keynesian doesn't mean he only studies macroeconomics.) Austrian economists certainly study macroeconomics—often zeroing in on how government economic policies produce unintended results, harming other groups that planners didn't think about, or harming the entire economy in the long run.

---

[17] So you can probably accurately predict that most buyers—if they had only two coat choices, of course—would pick the drab-but-warm gray one.
[18] Sandy Ikeda, "Broken-Windows Macroeconomics," Foundation for Economic Education, November 20, 2012, https://fee.org/articles/broken-windows-macroeconomics.

Price and Cost

As we saw a few pages back, scarcity forces us to choose from among limited resources to consume, as well as the type of work we want to do. **Prices** play a tremendously important part in determining what we will choose. These prices are in-finitely complicated and adjusted by millions of business owners *and* buyers.[19] A common fallacy claimed by those who favor fascist (government controlled) economies is that "Business owners are greedy! They can just charge the customers whatever they want; those customers are at the mercy of the business owners!"

But that's a ridiculous notion. If it were true, sellers would charge $1 million (or more) for a loaf of bread, and there would be little bread buyers could do about it. But you certainly already know those buyers *can* do several things about it: They can refuse to buy any bread (or buy less of it), they can bake it themselves, they can buy a substitute, or a combination of all those. The bread sellers would be forced to adjust their prices until they had enough buyers to make a profit, a decision they would have to make carefully, closely observing how much more or less that customers bought at each price change. **No group of government officials could possibly set prices as effectively as a voluntary-exchange system for even *one* item such as bread, much less for *millions* of goods and services!**

Supply, Demand, and Equilibrium

The pricing of items relates to the famous "law" of **supply and demand**. Supply, of course, describes how much of a good or service exists, and demand describes how much consumers want it. When supply and demand change, prices change. The "law" works this way: When demand increases for a product, the price increases. When demand decreases, the price decreases. When the supply (amount) of a product increases, the price decreases. When the supply of a product decreases, the price increases.

This is something that simply *happens* freely and predictably when governments leave buyers and sellers alone to make their own decisions. Something else also happens: Supply, demand, and prices reach a state of general **equilibrium**, or stability and balance. Here's how: Let's say a tire business opens in a small town, with no competing tire businesses. It's the only tire business within 50 miles, so everybody in the town who wants to buy a tire or have one fixed has little choice. The tire business owners realize this and charge a great deal of money for these services.

In a free economy, however, when others realize that the tire business owner is getting rich, guess what happens?

That's right: They go to his store and steal all his money.

---

[19] A **cost** is related to a price. For example, let's say that you have five dollars. You want to buy a loaf of bread (it's five dollars), and two pairs of socks (they're $2.50 each). You decide to buy the loaf of bread. The *price* of a loaf of bread is five dollars, but the *cost* of the loaf of bread is the two pairs of socks. (Remember the term **opportunity cost**?)

No, no, they don't do that (usually); instead, they open competing tire businesses. Do the new tire business owners charge as much as the original one? Hardly. If so, why bother to shop at the new stores? (Although some might go just to spite the original tire business owner, or just because it's closer.) But what happens is that the businesses begin to *compete*. Tire prices decrease. They fall until they reach a point at which the tire business owners decide that's as low as they can go and still make a satisfactory profit. That's the equilibrium.

Is this process perfectly logical and fair? Does it work with 100 percent accuracy? Of course not, but it's based upon the knowledge that the tire sellers *and* tire buyers have—*with both groups, as human beings consistently do, looking out for their own self-interests.* And that method works infinitely better than any a group of government planners could possibly come up with. Can you imagine a national Department of Tires, for example, run by a group of government officials, traveling around the nation, trying to determine how much tires and tire repair should cost in every city (with hundreds of sizes and types)?

...But we're getting ahead of ourselves—let's just stop right there and instead discuss one final economics term before we finish today:

Long-Term Ophiological Domestic Marginal Elasticity

(Do I hear a toddler crying somewhere?)

What Do You Think?

1. Briefly define these terms: *scarcity, opportunity cost, microeconomics, macroeconomics, Austrian economics, Keynesian economics, price, cost, supply, demand,* and *equilibrium.*
2. How do governments that try to run economies fail?
3. Explain how the price system relates to supply and demand.

3.3 – Money and Dividing Up Cows

How To Divide Up Cows

To begin this section, picture yourself as a resident of a charming little town during the Middle Ages. (Just try not to picture yourself in *too* much detail, since as a resident of the Middle Ages, you might not have bathed in 15 years.) And to keep this scenario simple, let's say that you and the other residents of this pleasant, happy little town are not currently dropping dead from the Black Plague.

Next, imagine that the residents of your little town do not use **money**—that is, a medium of exchange that everyone agrees upon. Instead, your fellow townspeople use a simple system of **barter**. In other words, they trade among themselves whatever goods and services they offer.

But the town's residents are tired of using barter; it's inconvenient and frustratting in a hundred different ways. Here are just two.

First, let's say that you're a carpenter, and an orange grove owner wants to trade with you, since he wants a table. But if you don't want or need oranges...you don't trade.

Second, it's hard to divide up many goods or services to make an even match during a trade. If you raise cattle, for example, and you want to trade for oranges...exactly how many oranges are equal to one cow? How does somebody measure something like that? And even if you and the orange grove owner *did* manage to agree that one cow is equal to, say, 200 oranges, what are you supposed to do if you don't *want* that many oranges?

A Surprise Visit

One beautiful morning in your lovely little medieval town, you look up happily at the clear, blue sky and feel the warm, golden sun as it shines brightly upon the 15 years' worth of dirt caked onto your face. Then you are stunned when you look down and see...*the queen*, who has just arrived for a surprise visit. As she passes by with her array of guards, Her Majesty suddenly turns to you and graciously says that she would be simply *delighted* not to have to throw you into a dungeon, provided you can come up with an idea for an item to be used in your country as a medium of exchange,

instead of just using barter. The queen also says that she wants this new medium of exchange item to have at least a few of these traits:
- The average person can carry it around conveniently.
- Buyers and sellers can easily divide it into "change," in case their trade isn't even.
- It's durable, so it can be used many, many times over many years without falling apart.
- It's scarce, so it has real value—not just something a person can find anywhere or create.
- It's useful for something other than currency, so everyone realizes that it's inherently valuable.

What Do You Think?

1. Write down several ideas on what you could use for a medium of exchange in this medieval town. Your idea(s) should fit all or most of the above requirements, or at least as many as possible. Bring these to class!
2. Fill in the blanks to finish these passages:
   - "If any would not ___, neither should he ___" (2 Thessalonians 3:10).
   - "No man can serve two ___...Ye cannot serve God and ___" (Jesus in Matthew 6:24).
   - "For no man ever hated ___; but nourisheth and cherisheth it" (Ephesians 5:29).

3.4 – Money, Weights, and Fraud • Quiz 3

Features of Money

Look at the ideas you came up with yesterday of items that could perform the job of an effective medium of exchange. What are those items' strengths and weaknesses as that medium?

Before the widespread use of money, barter was widely used. The growth of trade—that is, economic progress—using barter was slow, since, as we saw yesterday, barter's limitations are significant. For example, let's say a dairy farmer wants to trade with a carpenter for a table. But what is the dairy farmer supposed to do if neither that carpenter nor any other carpenter available to him wants any milk? Or what if no carpenter wants *enough* milk to be worth an entire table?

The history of money includes settling on a medium of exchange that is scarce, inherently valuable, and durable for use in many transactions. An effective medium can also be easily carried around and divided into change. Various items have been used throughout history as money, including shells, tobacco, whiskey, salt, cattle, spices, and in prisons...cigarettes! The medium that every society has consistently settled on, however, that fits these requirements, is precious metals—specifically, gold and silver. Here's why:

- They are scarce—they must be mined out of the earth, often with great labor, expense, and time (with no guarantee of success).
- They are divisible into weights of different sizes, to exchange for items of different value, in the form of bars, coins, or dust.
- They can be easily carried, even by small children.
- They last a long time—they won't rust, crumble, or dissolve.
- They have many other practical uses (jewelry, pacemakers, insulin pumps, conductors of heat and electricity to use in wiring, batteries, photography, computer chips, antibiotics, and space travel vehicles).

Mankind quickly recognized silver and gold's value. In fact, the Bible mentions their value many times, even as early as the book of Genesis, in which a river that went out of the Garden of Eden divided into four parts, one of which *"compasseth the whole land of Havilah, where there is gold; and the gold of that land is good"* (Genesis 2:11-12). And in Genesis 13:2, the Bible says Abram *"was very rich in cattle, in silver, and in gold."*

In later chapters we'll talk a little more about paper money, inflation, and other money-related topics. Let's focus now, however, on what government's proper role should be regarding money. Now, even if you didn't understand the sometimes-complicated aspects of banking, currency, money, inflation, and so on, by knowing and holding to the Biblical view of the role of government, you should be able to piece together a basic philosophy of how governments should be involved in money.

That said, to refresh your memory, mentally fill in the blanks of these Bible verses that discuss the purposes of government:

1. *Thus saith the Lord GOD; "Let it suffice you, O princes of Israel: remove ___ and ___, and execute ___ and ___" (Ezekiel 45:9).*

2. *Thus saith the LORD [to the king]; "Execute ye judgment and righteousness, and deliver the ___ out of the hand of the ___: and do no wrong, do no violence to the stranger, the fatherless, nor the widow, neither shed innocent blood in this place" (Jeremiah 22:3).*

3. *For rulers are not a ___ to good works, but to the ___....for he [the ruler] is the minister of God, a revenger to execute wrath upon him that doeth ___ (Romans 13:3-4).*

4. *Submit yourselves to every ordinance of man for the Lord's sake: whether it be to the king, as supreme; or unto governors, as unto them that are sent by him for the punishment of ___ (1 Peter 2:13-14).*

Government and Money

As mentioned, the reason that the subject of *government* keeps cropping up in an economics book is that throughout history, the subject of *economics* has been, unfortunately, closely tied up with government economic policies—nearly always *harmful* ones. And money is no different from any other topic when it comes to the Biblical role of government. The proper, Biblical role for government is to limit itself to threatening against and punishing violations of person and property, including fraud. For example, in matters involving money, governments should only get involved when buyers or sellers defraud others. Dishonest monetary weights, counterfeiting, and other types of attempts at *"spoil"* should unquestionably be *"remove[d]"* and punished by government. The Bible refers to that topic many times; a few examples follow (bold added):

- *"Thou shalt not **defraud** thy neighbor, neither **rob** him" (God in Leviticus 19:13).*
- *"Thou knowest the commandments, Do not commit adultery, Do not kill, Do not steal, Do not bear false witness, **Defraud not"** (Jesus in Mark 10:19).*
- *"**Just** balances, **just** weights, a **just** ephah, and a **just** hin[20] shall ye have" (God in Leviticus 19:35-36).*
- *A **false** balance is abomination to the LORD: but a **just** weight is his delight (Proverbs 11:1).*

Similar to what the Bible teaches on the subject, the true, moral role of government in money and banking has also been described this way:

> If the monetary unit is simply a unit of weight, then government's role in...money could well be confined to a simple Bureau of Weights and Measures, certifying this as well as other units of weight, length, or mass. The problem is that governments have systematically betrayed their trust as guardians of the precisely defined weight of the money commodity.[21]

What Do You Think?

1. To see the value of gold, complete this little project: (1) Look up the what the average yearly U. S. income was for the past year; (2) look up the current price of one ounce of gold, and (3) divide the yearly income amount in dollars by the number of dollars an ounce of gold is worth. How many ounces of gold could the average American buy for a year of work?

2. Answer "Yes" or "No" on whether a government that followed its proper, Biblical role should intervene in each of the five scenarios below:
    - A governor announces that only paper money printed by the state [the government] is to be allowed for buying and selling. →

---

[20] Ephahs and hins are units of measure.
[21] Murray Rothbard, *The Mystery of Banking* (The Ludwig von Mises Institute, 2008), 10.

- A seller claims that a buyer cheated him by paying him with "gold" coins that were actually half gold and half copper.
- A buyer says that a seller overcharged him for corn, because when the buyer weighed the 100 pounds of corn at home on *his* scale, the scale showed only 95 pounds of corn.
- A town legislature passes a law that limits the amount of interest that lenders may charge borrowers to 15 percent.
- A king decrees that all gold and silver coins must bear his official seal, to prevent counterfeiters from producing fake coins.

Take Quiz 3 (online or in-person students only). Feel free to use your notes, but there is a time limit!

(Next week, as you can see below, you will take Test 1 on Day 1.)

4.1 – Test 1

If you're in my in-person or online class, take Test 1 today. Review your notes for the first three weeks to prepare; this test is open notes. This test, and all others except the final, has 20 multiple-choice and/or matching questions and has a time limit. Do your best!

4.2 – Profit: Not a Bad Word at All

Scowling at Fat Cats

Somehow "profit" has transformed into a bad word. We're talking about *monetary* profit, of course, since we're discussing economics. In our day, so-called "social justice warriors" often practice a substitute religion of shrieking in protest against things they wrongly believe are immoral, without any real understanding of what they're protesting.

And *profit* is one of those things.

Because of relentless propaganda pushed by government schools, dishonest politicians, and most TV news re-porters, many poor, undiscerning souls scowl at the very mention of the word *profit*. And if they're not careful, even more sensible persons can get fooled by the strange notion that business owners—those pursuing a (Horrors!) *profit*—are all a bunch of evil, cack-ling, stout guys wearing top hats, smoking huge cigars, and blowing their noses on hundred-dollar bills wrapped around solid gold paper towel rolls.

But you won't be shocked to discover that thinking about the concept of profit that way is erroneous. Why?

Because <u>everybody</u> tries to profit in one way or another, in every transaction, either as a buyer or a seller.

We know from what the Bible teaches, and our everyday experiences—including knowing our own thoughts—that men and women seek what is best for themselves. Freedom for buyers and sellers to act in the way that they wish is how to best harness this self-preserving nature that we have.

And *profit* is the goal of that action.

The basic economic meaning of the word *profit* is the money you have left over after you meet your expenses. A furniture store owner, for example, might in a month sell $25,000 of furniture; this is called **gross** sales. But if that store owner's expenses that month amount to $20,000 (what *he* paid for the furniture, rent, salaries, insurance, cleaning, taxes, and so on), his **net** income is $5,000.

A more general definition for the noun *profit* is, as Webster's Dictionary puts it, "any gain or pecuniary [monetary] advantage...any advantage...the acquisition of anything valuable." Webster defines the verb *profit* as "to benefit; to advantage...to improve; to advance."[22]

In a voluntary economy, persons profit by exchanging goods and services, or exchanging money for them. Let's say a woman buys a loaf of bread for $3. When we observe that exchange, we tend to think this:

*The bread seller sure **profited** from that transaction.*

But that's only half the truth! Why?

*Because the bread **buyer** also profited,* since she valued the loaf of bread more than she valued the $3 that she gave for it.

And that's the classic definition of the term *profit*: **a benefit or an advantage**. You could say the same thing about those who buy haircuts or bicycles. Those buyers *profit* from those exchanges, since acquiring those goods or services—haircuts that make them look nicer, or bicycles that help them get around more easily—is more important to them than the money they used to buy them.

---

[22] *Webster's Dictionary 1828: American Dictionary of the English Language*, "Profit," https://webstersdictionary1828.com/Dictionary/profit.

And it's not only millionaires and billionaires who seek profit. It's the computer repair shop owner down the street. It's the guy with a lawn care business who worships with you. It's the homeschooling mom who makes and sells essential oils. It's the teenaged young lady who works at a restaurant that sells chicken sandwiches with two pickles on them. And...it's even the Christian missionaries who give up well-paid careers or other benefits to reach the lost in a remote village.

Yes, those missionaries are seeking profit!

The difference? They're aiming to store up for themselves treasure in heaven by becoming missionaries, because they believe that path *profits* them better than spending more of their time striving for more earthly profits. (Of course, this is not the same thing as saying that those missionaries are greedily seeking after their own selves.)

What Profits Can Do

To restate, because of the anti-freedom mentality of many today, the average person gets a twisted, incomplete, and inaccurate picture of profits, imagining them as something pursued only by millionaires who think of nothing except greedily scraping for another dollar, 24 hours a day.

Incidentally, this is often a comforting, satisfying feeling for those who believe it, since they can contentedly bask in this thought:

> *Look what a great, morally superior person **I** am!* ***I'm*** *certainly not a money-grubber like that **profiteer** over there!*[23]

But profits play a key role in civilization. Here are just three:

1. **Profits enable others to earn a living.** A person who starts a for-profit business often hires others to help run it. Those employees can now provide for themselves and their families, *all because an until-then total stranger was trying to make a profit*. And what happens to hiring when a business owner makes even *greater* profits? You guessed it!

2. **Profits ensure that the goods and services that people want are available.** When a certain type of business is profitable, it means that consumers want to buy what that business is selling. That signals to others that if they want to join in on the profits, they should open similar businesses. The result? The goods and services that consumers want are more available.

3. **Profits increase the standard of living, which especially helps the poor.** When a shoemaker enjoys profits, he can invest them in new machines or other technologies that help him make shoes more efficiently (and therefore, more cheaply). When these shoes cost him less to make, he can charge less. What do his competitors then have to do to keep up with him? That's right: They must invest in technol-

---

[23] By the way, do you see how those who think that way *profit* from that thought?

ogy themselves. And how do shoe buyers benefit from this? They're able to buy more with their money.

Thousands of goods and services that are readily available and relatively cheap today—smart phones, cars, air conditioning, indoor plumbing, electric lights, refrigerators, computers, and so on—were at first far too costly for poor and middle-class families to buy. I'm old enough to remember that VCRs—video cassette recorders, which played movies on tapes before DVD players, Blu-ray players, and DVRs replaced them—cost around $2,000 when they first came out.[24] Only the very richest families had them, and it was amazing to be able to go to a (very rich) friend's house and watch a movie on his TV, without having to pay for a movie ticket at the theater. But thanks to *profit*, those items, and many others like them, became affordable for billions of consumers.

(And this doesn't even take into account how beneficial to mankind the role that profit has played in making critical items like good food, clean water, medical care, and clothing more available to the average person.)

That's why it is absolutely ridiculous to see some grouchy, ungrateful malcontent holding up a sign that says something like "GET RID OF SELFISH PROFITEERS," while texting a message on a high-tech phone, wearing comfortable and relatively inexpensive clothing and shoes, having just exited a grocery store that offers 257 varieties of gluten-free cheese, getting into a comfortable air-conditioned import car...and driving to a job provided by business owners who (a) took a gigantic risk with their life savings to start that business, and (b) still work like dogs to make sure it is successful.

What Those Evil Rich Guys Do with Their Money

And let's just say, for the sake of argument, that some "rich guy" makes "too much profit"—that is, according to somebody *else's* definition of what is "too much." What does Mr. Evil Rich Guy *do* with his profits, after he pays his taxes and all his other expenses?

Well, he certainly doesn't stuff all his money under a mattress. He doesn't drain his swimming pool, fill the empty pool with his money, and then dive into the middle of the piles of bills, throwing them up into the air and screaming with glee. He doesn't take the bills and stitch them together into blankets to cover himself up while he sleeps.

Instead, *he uses his profits to buy many goods and services and invest in other businesses!*

And what happens when he buys something—say, an item that only those Evil Rich Guys buy, like a fancy new yacht, which might gain him ever deeper scowls from the anti-profit crowd? Well, even if Mr. Evil Rich Guy buys a yacht, he is still benefiting society by providing jobs to those who help manufacture yachts: lumber and plastic and metal producers, carpenters, boat builders, glass makers, carpet manufacturers, engine builders, electronics manufacturers, painters, office painters and cleaners, yacht repairmen, and many others.

---

[24] This is equivalent to about $10,000 today.

And if Mr. Evil Rich Guy *invests* his profits, he risks losing it—*every penny of it*—which means wiping out the benefit of potentially hundreds or thousands of hours' worth of work. But let's say his investment pays off; in what kind of company might he invest? Of course, he might invest in an immoral company, like a gambling joint or a movie corporation that produces gory films.

But...maybe Mr. E. R. Guy will invest in a company that's working to develop a more secure car seatbelt that will save lives.

Or maybe he'll invest in an engineer who's developed a farming machine that produces crops more efficiently, makes food cheaper for millions, and helps the poor more easily afford healthful food.

Or maybe he'll invest in a doctor who has discovered a new type of surgery to save the lives of those who would otherwise die.

And what in the world is wrong with that?

Government Meddlers, Cronies, and Consumer Bosses

Many politicians—who make a very *profitable* living being employed at taxpayer expense—are among the first to wail about and try to punish those whom they label "greedy profiteers." One famous example occurred under Franklin D. Roosevelt, who was U. S. President from 1933 to 1945, when the U. S. government raised taxes on "excess profits."[25] As if any government official knows exactly how much profit a business ought to make and can point to a number which is an "excess profit"! Can you imagine the gall of those who think they know what this number is? Do government officials have a special crystal ball they can gaze into that tells them precisely when the profit that a total stranger makes is "excess"?

Incredible.

```
                EXCESS-PROFITS TAX


                    MESSAGE
                       FROM
       THE PRESIDENT OF THE UNITED STATES
                    TRANSMITTING
    RECOMMENDATION FOR THE ENACTMENT OF A STEEPLY
    GRADUATED EXCESS-PROFITS TAX, TO BE APPLIED TO ALL
    INDIVIDUALS AND ALL CORPORATE ORGANIZATIONS WITHOUT
    DISCRIMINATION.


    JULY 1, 1940.—Referred to the Committee on Ways and Means and ordered to
                           be printed
```

---

[25] Jim Powell, "How FDR's New Deal Harmed Millions of Poor People," *The Cato Institute*, December 29, 2003, cato.org/commentary/how-fdrs-new-deal-harmed-millions-poor-people.

In a free-exchange economy, you know who dictates how much profit that a company makes?

Consumers.

Those consumers can make or break a company at any time, simply by buying that company's product, or by *not* buying it. And there's no guarantee that a profitable company will *stay* profitable; even successful companies must adapt and listen to customers—*and please those customers*—to stay in business. (Scores of companies that made millions year after year have gone bankrupt after failing to keep up with changing consumer demands.) When a government doesn't try to run an economy, the customer is king.

One type of company, however, does deserve contempt from those who sup-port limited, moral government: the type of company that makes profits by us-ing the government's power to force consumers to pay for its product or service. One subcategory of That Type of Business is the company that arranges to get a law passed that protects it from competition. Some companies do this by getting tariffs (taxes on imports) added to competing foreign goods, so buyers are forced to pay more for products they could have bought for less. Another subcategory of That Type of Business is one that arranges to have a law passed that requires consumers to buy their product. One example of this type is drug companies that influence lawmakers to pressure everyone to get many vaccines and other injections. Another relatively recent example is the famous "Obamacare" law that forced many Americans to buy health insurance whether they wanted it or not.

What Profits Can't Do

To finish this section, let's focus on several other things we should keep in mind about profit:

> *Riches profit not in the day of wrath: but righteousness delivereth from death (Proverbs 11:4).*
>
> *In all labor there is profit: but the talk of the lips tendeth only to penury [poverty] (Proverbs 14:23).*
>
> *"For what shall it profit a man, if he shall gain the whole world, and lose his own soul?" (Jesus in Mark 8:36).*

In other words, first, riches won't help a sinner avoid the judgment of God. Second, if you want to make a better living, you should work more and talk less. Finally, what a waste of a life it is to spend it getting riches, if you spend eternity without God!

What Do You Think?

1. Define "profit" just as a general term, then as an economics term.
2. How is profit a universal goal among humans? →

3. Why do you think so many today say they're against profit? How do their own actions contradict their claim?
4. Explain several ways that profit helps communities and advances civilization. What is absurd about government attempts to punish "excess profits"?
5. How is a Christian's view of profit different?

4.3 – Capitalism: Mutual, Voluntary, and Beneficial

Another Non-Bad Word

The now-famous term **capitalism** is believed to have first been used in 1850 by French socialist Louis Blanc. Blanc used it as an insult, and German philosopher Karl Marx used the term as a term of disgust in his 1867 book *Das Kapital*. This sneering take on the term prevails in many places, which makes capitalism appear evil and oppressive. Anti-capitalists such as Marx, Blanc, and many university professors and government school teachers have deceived/still deceive others into believing that only two choices exist:

Anti-Capitalist Propaganda Poster

Fake Choice #1: The first choice, they say, is that a nation can operate under *capitalism*.[26] By that, they mean a system run by evil (huge, cigar-smoking) businessmen. These businessmen—according to critics of *capitalism*—don't do any actual work themselves; they just own and direct all the **capital**—machines, factories, money, tools, and other items used to produce goods and services. According to this warped view of the "system," workers are stuck as slaves to *capitalists* for the rest of their lives.

Fake Choice #2: The other choice, anti-capitalists say, is a glorious system in which laborers gloriously own everything, combined with a glorious government that controls businesses through the brilliant and unselfish (and glorious) efforts of government planners to make everyone happy through shared wealth, which is, as you have probably guessed, glorious.

---

[26] These individuals pronounce the word "CAP-italism" in the same tone you would use to say the word "HIT-ler."

• • • • •

Those who believe in the right for humans to work and buy and sell as they choose see those two choices as utterly ridiculous. Those who love liberty sometimes prefer to use a term like **voluntary cooperation** instead of "capitalism." They reject the weird idea that there are fixed groups of capitalists and laborers forever chiseled in stone. As history has shown endless times under voluntary cooperation, individuals can—and do—build up wealth, change jobs, and increase their standard of living.

> **In fact, a voluntary-exchange system, which some call "capitalism," *isn't really a "system" at all*. It's "run" by millions of individual buyers and sellers making billions of daily—and imperfect—decisions in their own self-interest.**

This contrasts drastically to socialism, which *is* an actual system of thieving, oppressive laws that a government thunders down upon its often-unwilling citizens. (We'll talk more about socialism in the next chapter.)

Now, why on earth would any sane person *oppose* a system in which all were free to pursue their own interests without state interference, as long as they didn't steal from or harm others?

Well, it's hard to argue that a *sane* person would, but there are reasons why some oppose voluntary exchange. Some critics of "capitalism" are simply jealous of those who are (a) ingenious enough to figure out how to satisfy the wants and needs of many consumers (and hard enough workers to produce those things), and (b) rewarded with profits by doing so. Other critics of capitalism are ignorant of how a free society and voluntary exchange could work. *Those critics wrongly believe that the only way someone gains economically (that is, makes profits) is by **taking** from others, making them poorer—instead of gaining wealth by **serving** others' wants and needs. In other words, those critics don't understand that "capitalists" in a free, voluntary-exchange system profit **by profiting others**.*

And remember, we know from the Bible's teachings—and our own eyes and ears—that human beings act in their own self-interest. A voluntary system of exchange simply employs this tendency and directs it toward the benefit of society. How? Again, by rewarding individuals for meeting the needs and wants of *other* consumers.

Answering Critics of Voluntary Exchange ("Capitalism")

Anti-capitalist critics often trot out several complaints about That Horrible System of Capitalism. Here are three common ones, each with a short response that follows:

1. **"Capitalism is a vicious system of 'survival of the fittest,' where businesses try to beat each other through cutthroat competition."**

"Well, the competition you're talking about is true, for sure. And sometimes if a business can't compete, it folds up. But you're just looking at *one* side of the story. When businesses compete, they do it by offering lower prices, faster service, and better products. And that's great for consumers! Nobody wants a business to fail, obviously. But if it does, it's because buyers exercising their right to choose what to buy led to that business's closing. Wait a minute...I thought I saw you protesting the other day that we should all have 'the right to choose'; are you saying that you're *against* that now?"

"That's a whole different subject."

"Would you like to *talk* about that subject?"

"Not right now."

"And wait a minute...you're an evolutionist, aren't you?"

"Yeah, so what?"

"Well, you're complaining about capitalism's being a system run by 'survival of the fittest.' You believe in evolution—in the 'survival of the fittest,' right? Then why do you think it's wrong if *businesses* fiercely compete against each other, and some go 'extinct'?"

2. **"Capitalists abuse workers and cheat the poor."**

"No decent person makes excuses when somebody abuses somebody else, obviously. But in a truly free voluntary system of exchange, you don't have to work for anybody you don't want to work for; you can quit any time. And the same goes for buying things; if you don't like a company, you don't have to buy its products. And with a just government, any criminal abuses or fraud from employers would be addressed and punished. Besides, a voluntary 'system' that allows all individuals to make their own choices on buying and selling and working and quitting and hiring shouldn't be blamed for those who try to cheat or steal from others, should it? People are *individuals*! Let's sic the law on *just the ones who violate the rights of others*, not everybody else."

3. **"Capitalism encourages people to be *selfish*."**

"Actually, in a voluntary-exchange economic system, a person gains wealth by making *others* happy. If you open a restaurant, for example, your food had better taste good and be reasonably priced if you want customers to come back. If you're a doctor, you'd better do an excellent job at helping patients recover and/or reducing their pain. If you sell phones, they'd better be convenient, reliable, and easy to use if you want to sell a lot of them.

"And I'm assuming we're not talking about businesses that try to use the government's power to *force* others to be customers. That's clearly wrong. And as far as those like you who criticize so-called 'capitalism,' Austrian economist Ludwig von Mises wisely pointed out this:

All people, however fanatical they may be in their zeal to disparage [criticize] and to fight capitalism, implicitly [indirectly] pay homage [respect] to it by passionately clamoring for the products it turns out.[27]

Capitalism and Christianity

Pure capitalism doesn't exist anywhere on earth, and it never has. Even in a nation like America, federal, state, county, and city governments place literally tens of thousands of frustrating and needless obstacles and regulations in the way of those who simply want to buy and sell so they can profit themselves (while profiting others as well). But even if a "pure" economy based on voluntary exchange somehow got put into place, flaws would still exist, because (a) humans  are sinful and act sinfully; and (b) consumers and producers don't know everything, and this lack of knowledge can cause them to make "wrong" economic decisions.

But what's the alternative? An economic system like socialism or communism, in which government planners decide for millions of individuals what they're allowed to produce, buy, and sell—and how much they're allowed to charge and pay for those goods and services? Any sensible person must realize that this idea is utter madness. Here's how von Mises put it:

All rational action is in the first place individual action. Only the individual thinks. Only the individual reasons. Only the individual acts.[28]

In a voluntary-exchange "system," is there greed? Of course there is! If we know what the Bible says about man—and have our eyes and ears even half open—we're not surprised at all about this. But as we've seen, a voluntary system rewards the "greedy" when...they provide things that *others* want. Think about it: People in a voluntary-exchange system can get rich by providing clothes, homes, food, soap, hot water, and a million other goods and services to *total strangers*. Business owners, for example, can make a living by helping to clothe and feed children they've never even met!

In fact, voluntary exchange also makes it possible for you to have time to read this book, rather than having to work 14 hours a day so you can earn enough money to contribute to your family's food budget. The freedom to benefit from farming inventions made food cheaper for billions, and it allowed them to spend many fewer hours working each week to get it. Voluntary exchange also enhances culture, since individuals who may work fewer hours per

---

[27] Ricardo Salinas, "Capitalism Is Here to Stay. The Challenge Is Making It a Part of Our Society's Societal Commitment," Aspen Institute, June 16, 2017, aspeninstitute.org/blog-posts/capitalism-stay-challenge-making-part-societys-social-commitment.
[28] Ludwig von Mises, *Socialism: An Economic and Sociological Analysis* (New Haven, Yale University Press, 1951), 113.

day to survive therefore have a total of billions of more hours to paint, write, compose music, invent, and study glorious, *glorious* economics. And in a (somewhat) free economy like the U. S., for example, many other benefits exist we hardly think about.

Here's just one: In the U. S. (and other relatively economically free nations, of course) you can go to practically any restaurant or grocery store, and even without buying *anything*, use a restroom that is relatively clean and almost certainly has hot water, soap, paper towels, and...everything else. It probably isn't as clean and convenient as your bathroom at home (I hope), but it's most likely better than nearly all kings or millionaires had in the history of the world up until 150 years or so ago. In poorer, less advanced nations with no history of a voluntary exchange system, on the other hand, only the wealthiest individuals have easy and free access to conveniences like this. And in nations like the U. S., which is, again, only *partly* "capitalistic," those who are truly hungry can go into a grocery store and ask a manager for leftover or day-old food, and they'll almost always be accommodated at little cost—or *no* cost.

Another Anti-Capitalist Propaganda Poster

One reason why the (partially) capitalistic system in America has worked is because of the influence of Christianity upon its culture, or at least, a culture in which much of the public believed in a God and was therefore respectful—generally—of private property, honesty, and hard work, although this outlook is shrinking. In his 1904 book *The Protestant Ethic and the Spirit of Capitalism*, German author Max Weber points out that because of Christianity's influence, European capitalism developed comparatively *morally*, by encouraging honesty and frowning upon lying, as opposed to a viewpoint of extolling con artists as crafty and smart when they ripped off others.[29]

For example, in America for many decades it was easy to find—in front of a grocery store, to name one location—a newspaper vending machine that

---

[29] Daniel Natal, "Christianity and Capitalism," February 15, 2022, The Daniel Natal Show, youtube.com/watch?v=Lp4aoj6dM7g.

opened if a customer put in exact change for a copy. It wasn't hard at all for customers to put in the correct change for a single paper, open the machine, and take *all* the newspapers. But this kind of theft rarely happened.[30] One current decades-old-but-still-common phenomenon in this country is ordering a drink and a meal at a non-fast-food restaurant, eating and drinking it, and only paying the bill and leaving a tip *after* finishing the meal. Do some restaurant customers sneak out without paying? Sure, some do, but when that happens, it's an aberration.

Christianity and a voluntary-exchange economy are great partners!

(And obviously, you don't have to be a Christian to honestly pay for your meal or take only the newspaper that you've paid for, but without question the influence of Christianity contributes to a culture of honesty and respect for the property of others.)

The magnificence and the value of the voluntary system of exchange is so fascinating and beautiful that it's worth just sitting and thinking about for hours and hours, especially when it's your turn to do the dishes. Think about all the incredible conveniences we enjoy today; why do we enjoy them? Because "our" government doesn't *totally* block individuals' attempts to benefit themselves...**by producing goods and services that *others* want.**

Is it getting clearer to you on how the Bible is exactly right again about the nature of man, economics, and government's true purpose?

What Do You Think?

1. How is actual "capitalism" (a) not what its critics say it is, and (b) not even a real *system*?
2. Sum up the responses to the three anti-capitalist arguments given.
3. What does capitalism provide for a nation, and for individuals?
4. What foundation does Christianity provide for capitalism? What do the examples of the newspaper vending machine and restaurant bill mean to you?

4.4 – Socialism, Part 1: Immoral and Anti-Christian

Can We Be Left Alone?

Do you have a strong urge to grab all of your friends, convince them to sell everything they have, move to a huge piece of property, and share all your labor and possessions equally with each other?

---

[30] In college I worked with a woman who lived outside the U. S. for many years, and once she told me how fascinated she was that people in America didn't just take *all* the newspapers from the vending machines when they put in only enough coins for one! She said that where she lived, if that kind of newspaper machine existed, it would be stolen clean in a matter of minutes with a person who put in coins for just one paper.

You *do*? Fine! Go right ahead and do it; nobody's stopping you. But those of us who *don't* want to participate in that kind of setup would like to say from the bottom of our hearts: "Leave us alone."

But that's not how many socialists and communists see things. Not only do they hold to a belief in a system that runs counter to all human nature and experience, they often think they also have the right to *force* everybody else using the power of the law to *join* them in their madness.

"Hammer and Sickle" Symbol of Communism

First, let's quickly define **socialism**. It's an economic system in which a government with broad powers takes over and/or heavily regulates businesses. That government also tries to determine what items and how many/ much of those items should be produced, passes laws to "spread the wealth" (by plundering the "rich"), and hassles those with property.

Communism is even worse; that system does all of the above socialist system, *and* its ruling class threatens, fines, jails, tortures, and murders those who resist, or even speak out against it. Communists are "inspired" by *The Communist Manifesto*, an 1848 essay by German philosopher Karl Marx (1818-1883). In *The Communist Manifesto*, Marx viewed history as a struggle between two groups. The first group he called the **bourgeoisie**, or what he saw as an elite ruling class that owned all the *capital*: land, machinery, factories, money, and other elements of producing goods and services. The second group he called the **proletariat**; these, Marx said, are laborers who work for the bourgeoisie.

Karl Marx

Marx made it seem as if these two groups were set in stone, and that no one could ever change from one group to the other. He apparently was completely unaware of the millions who had lifted themselves—or had been lifted by the efforts of others—out of poverty, thanks to free markets and voluntary cooperation among buyers and sellers. But that's probably being generous; it's hard to believe that Marx didn't know that this was and had been happening in America and other places in the world. It seems likely, therefore, that he was being disingenuous. Marx claimed in *The Communist Manifesto* that after the State (government) took control of all the machines, factories, and land used to produce goods, mankind's progress would lead it into a glorious, perfect socialist state, which would transition finally and totally into *voluntary* communism. *But how would this communist state first get control over materials owned by "capitalists"?* Here's how, says Marx:

> The proletariat will...wrest [seize], by degrees, all capital from the bourgeoisie, to centralize all instruments of production in the hands of the State, i.e., of the proletariat organized as the ruling class; and to increase the total of productive forces as rapidly as possible. Of course, in the be-

ginning, this cannot be effected except by means of despotic inroads on [tyrannical theft of] the rights of property.[31]

Did you see how Marx taught that all property should be taken from "capitalists"? He said it should be done "by means of despotic inroads"—that is, *by an all-powerful State that violently steals this property.* How ironic that **every time communism is put into practice, a group of powerful tyrants rules over a nation's people, impoverishing and violently abusing them**—the exact scenario that Marx claimed he was trying to *prevent*!

A Moral Failure

Today we'll focus on socialism instead of communism, since it's less trendy these days to declare your love for communism. Sure, socialism *sounds* less threatening, and it comes across as compassionate to support an economic system that has a reputation—at least to the ignorant—as fair and benevolent. But socialism has miserably failed every time it's been tried—except for the ones who get to *run* those socialist states, or those connected to the rulers. They get fabulously wealthy, never suffering like the ones being subjected to the socialist system. As noted yesterday, critics of "capitalism" often oppose it because they claim that it encourages "selfishness." And socialists—the ones who haven't had to *live* under socialism, that is—can console themselves by stating or thinking something like this:

> *I'm so **caring** and concerned about the poor! **I'm** not greedy like those selfish **capitalists** who just try to pile up more **money** every day.*

But as economics professor Dr. Thomas Sowell reasonably points out:

> I have never understood why it is "greed" to want to keep the money you have earned, but not greed to want to take somebody else's money.[32]

Socialism's moral and logical failings are many; here are just a few. First, it ignores mankind's natural tendency to please himself. Instead of taking advantage of this bent, socialism *punishes* it by regulating and taxing those who produce goods and services, discouraging them from *wanting* to produce more. Socialism also rewards the rich and the powerful and hurts the poor. The system of government control encourages businesses to take advantage of this control to bribe or blackmail lawmakers to arrange for *their* businesses to be the ones which the State favors and rewards.[33] Also, socialist leaders always get rich from plundering the people, while most of the nation they rule ends up poorer, if not in total poverty. And because a system of socialism severely retards economic growth, *it hurts the poor the worst*, since an economy grows

---

[31] Wikisource, *Manifesto of the Communist Party*, https://en.wikisource.org/wiki/Page:Manifesto_of_the_Communist_Party.djvu/45.
[32] Thomas Sowell, *Barbarians at the Gate and Other Controversial Essays* (Hoover Institution Press, 2020).
[33] This, of course, can and does occur in "capitalistic" economies and governments too.

National Socialist (Nazi) Party Symbol

partly by finding ways to produce goods more affordably. When those gains are *not* made, fewer families are lifted out of poverty.

That last issue is why many reasonable individuals are infuriated to hear socialists absurdly claim that they support the poor and oppose "rich and powerful and greedy *capitalists*." "Powerful?" Well, it's true that wealthy entrepreneurs—in an economy that allows buyers and sellers to pursue their own best interests—are "powerful"...in that they've made a great deal of money by pleasing others, who reward them by willingly and happily paying them for their products and services. But in a voluntary-exchange "system," those wealthy entrepreneurs could go bankrupt if they failed to satisfy consumers. Contrast that to a socialist nation, in which dangerously powerful officials decide the futures of others. Or in a communist nation, where officials wield the additional power to be able to jail or *murder* those who resist or even *disagree* with them.

Punishing those who make money by serving others?
Stealing profits through destructive taxation?
Piling on endless regulations on businesses?
Now *that's* power. Why don't socialists complain about *that*?

Christians and Socialism

Some philosophers today—often ones who couldn't care less what God's Word says about any *other* topic—suddenly appear to develop a deep interest in the Bible when they imagine and proclaim that it supports socialism. But we've already seen that (a) God's Word has a specific explanation of what the *true* purposes of government are, and they don't include creating and running a socialist economy; and (b) the Bible affirms many times the right to private property. But critics of this view will point to Bible passages like this:

> *And all that believed [in Jesus Christ] were together, and had all things common; and sold their possessions and goods, and parted them to all men, as every man had need. And the multitude of them that believed were of one heart and of one soul: neither said any of them that ought of the things which he possessed was his own; but they had all things common (Acts 2:44-45).*

> *And with great power gave the apostles witness of the resurrection of the Lord Jesus: and great grace was upon them all. Neither was there any among them that lacked: for as many as were possessors of lands or houses sold them, and brought the prices of the things that were sold, and laid them down at the apostles' feet: and distribution was made unto every man according as he had need (Acts 4:33-35).*

Of course, both passages describe a *voluntary* sharing of possessions among followers of Jesus, not a *mandatory* economic system in which the government forces both believers and unbelievers to share their money and their property.

That kind of forced system, by the way, would (a) be totally impractical, and (b) violate the clear Biblical guidelines of government's proper functions. Christians, as well as to anybody else who can think rationally, should oppose socialism as an economic system for many reasons, including these four: (1) It has never worked. (2) It *can't* possibly work, since it denies the fact that mankind has a self-seeking nature. (3) It ends up robbing from the poor and giving to the rich, because the rich wield power or strongly influence those in power. (And giving the rich more power over the poor is exactly what socialists always claim to *oppose*!) (4) It turns the moral purpose of the law upside down by *stealing* property and *violating* the people's liberties, instead of *protecting* property and *upholding* the people's liberties.

What Do You Think?

1. Explain some of the moral failures of socialism. Can you think of any others that weren't listed?
2. Why do some claim that Christianity teaches socialism as a preferred economic system? How is socialism incompatible with Christianity?

5.1 – Socialism, Part 2: Irrational and Unworkable

Let's continue looking at socialism. Today we'll focus on why it is an unworkable system—even dangerous and deadly. Government planners running a socialistic economic system lack the ability to make economic decisions effectively and accurately for others. And those officials' hostility toward private property—except their *own* private property, of course—makes it virtually impossible to employ socialism to satisfy consumers' nearly infinite wants, and more importantly, *needs*.

You Want To Be a Central Planner? We Have Questions First!

Socialism always fails—that is, except for government leaders and politically-connected businesses, who use their authority and influence to make themselves rich **at the expense of others**, who become poorer.

And to repeat: Empowering the rich and hurting the poor are two things that socialists always *claim* that they're *against*!

Many nations over the past century—China, Russia, Nicaragua, Vietnam, Venezuela, North Korea, etc.—have tried socialism or communism; every attempt failed—or *is* failing.[34] One key reason socialism fails, to repeat, is that it

---

[34] Rainer Zitelman, "Socialism: The Failed Idea That Never Dies," *Forbes*, March 16, 2020, forbes.com/sites/rainerzitelmann/2020/03/16/socialism-the-failed-idea-that-never-dies.

is utterly impossible for a group of planners to predict or plan out what goods and services millions of individuals will choose to buy or sell, in what quantities, and for what prices. Therefore, we have some questions for all those Wannabe Central Planners (WCPs):

1. **Haven't you ever heard of socialism's failures?** If you haven't, why not? How can you consider yourselves qualified to "run an economy" if you're still ignorant of these planned economies and their horrible failures, causing so much human poverty, misery, and death? If you *have* heard of socialism's failures, why don't you care about those who have suffered and are suffering under those systems, as well as those who *will* suffer under yours? And what makes you think that you and your fellow WCPs are smarter than every other group that tried it before?

2. **What gives you the right to make economic decisions for everybody?** Do you and other WCPs have some special knowledge that no one else on earth has? If you say, "Yes," were you *born* with this special knowledge? Or did you *learn* it somewhere? If you answered "Yes" to either one of those questions, where's the *proof* that you have this knowledge? Did you take a test to demonstrate that you had it? If so, what were the questions on this test? And how does everyone else know the creators and graders of this test created and graded it correctly? Is there someone checking *them* to make sure they did so? And why can't *I* and others I know take this test? Maybe we'll score higher on it than you and your fellow WCPs did![35]

3. **Aren't you aware of the many other routine failures that always occur when governments run things?** This includes government schools that spend hundreds of billions of dollars every year, with worse and worse results; the incompetency and excruciating slowness of agencies like the Department of Motor Vehicles; and potholes on government-maintained roads that don't get fixed for months or years—if ever.

4. **How do you calculate the endless variables when you "spread the wealth"?** That is, how do you decide how much each family should get per month in, say, medical care? What about younger persons who are healthy? How about those with diseases or bigger families? What about those who cause their own health problems by alcohol or drug abuse, gluttony, an inactive lifestyle, and/or smoking? What are the *exact* formulas you use to determine how much to "give" each family, if you *do* have any? And if you do, how do you know the formulas are correct? Did you have a team of angels from heaven, or at least, mathematicians or financial experts, look them over?

---

[35] Frederic Bastiat asks government meddlers similar questions in *The Law*.

5. **Have you ever heard of Adam Smith?** In his book *The Wealth of Nations*, he wrote, *"The statesman who should attempt to direct private people in what manner they ought to employ their capitals* [what they should buy, sell, and invest in, and how to use the materials they own to produce goods and services], *would...assume an authority which could safely be trusted, not only to no single person, but to no council or senate whatever, and which would nowhere be so dangerous as in the hands of a man who had folly and presumption enough to fancy himself fit to exercise it."* In other words, only those who are arrogant beyond belief or complete *kooks* with no self-awareness would ever in a million years think that they were talented enough to "run an economy." Are you and your fellow WCPs the exception to this? If your answer is "Yes," how do we *know* that? Can you *prove* that somehow? And will you explain to all of us who aren't gifted with your magical knowledge *why* you believe Adam Smith was wrong about this point?

Those questions are so obvious—especially since socialism has failed *every single time* it's been tried—that it's also fair to ask WCPs this question:

> Why are you *still* pushing socialism on "your" nation? You've *got* to know that it never works, and surely you know it won't work *this* time, either. So what are you trying to do—loot taxpayers and make yourselves and your friends rich with the spoil?

This last question becomes especially appropriate, since any sensible person must realize that these Wannabe Central Planners can't be *totally* ignorant of socialism's track record of utter failure. And the fact that they always claim that they're against "the rich"...yet in socialist or communist systems, *a rich, privileged class always rules*, even as others in the system suffer all around them, makes it infuriating. "We're against the rich and powerful!" Yeah, sure you are.

Impossible to Succeed

In *Human Action*, his 1949 work on man, government, and economics, Ludwig von Mises offers this devastating critique of central planners:

> The paradox of "planning" is that it cannot plan, because of the absence of economic calculation. What is called a planned economy is no economy at all. It is just a system of groping about in the dark. There is no question of a rational choice of means for the best possible attainment of the ultimate ends sought. What is called conscious planning is precisely the elimination of conscious purposive action.[36]

In other words, in a socialist/communist economic system, central planners cannot *possibly* figure out what kinds of goods and services—hundreds of thousands, if not *millions* of them!—should be produced, or in what quantities, or how much they should cost, or how often they should be produced. In Amer-

---

[36] Ludwig von Mises, *Human Action* (Yale University Press, 1949), 696.

ica, for example, 100 million or more buyers and sellers make *billions* of these decisions daily. Buyers make the best choices they can, given the information they have; sellers do the same.

What happens if *buyers* of goods and services make mistakes? Well, they hurt their own economic situations by spending too much money, buying too much or too little of a product, buying a poor-quality product, and so on. They have every incentive to *avoid* these types of mistakes.

And what happens if *sellers* make similar mistakes? They think and work and sweat and strain to produce goods and services that consumers want. They also try hard not to make errors in these decisions, such as how much of a product to manufacture; whether they should keep manufacturing what they're already making, or if they ought to switch to producing a *different* product; or how much they can charge for it (and how much is too much, so they don't lose buyers). Sellers are also faced with this serious and urgent incentive: If they make mistakes in these types of decisions, their businesses could fail; they could go bankrupt; and they could lose their savings, homes, and future financial security. What's the point of spelling all of this out? The point is this (make sure you understand this!):

> ***Individuals* can face serious personal consequences if they make mistakes in their buying, producing, and selling decisions. But <u>those who run a socialist economy face little or no personal consequences</u> if *their* economic decisions for a nation are dead wrong.**

What if central planners wrongly decide, for example, on the number of carrots that "should" be grown one season? Or the number of cars that "should" be built this year? Or how many pairs of blue jeans that "should" be produced? Do those planners lose their jobs or their homes or their savings?

Nope.

Contrast that to a farmer who could suffer greatly if he miscalculates on the number of acres he uses to grow carrots as a crop during one season. He has every incentive *not* to make a mistake; central planners have none. And how do you think it turns out when planners know that *no matter how irresponsible or wrong their decisions are, they'll almost never have to face consequences for their blunders*?

You won't be surprised at all to learn that socialist regimes are also infamous for creating problematic, frustrating situations in which, for example, every grocery store has shelves overflowing with jars of pickled beets (because that's what central planners decided that farmers should grow, and others should can)...but those same stores lack important items like toothpaste, light bulbs, or soap.

Socialist rulers make these shortages even worse when they tax and regulate away the *incentive* of those who might want to, for example, produce more toothpaste. In a voluntary-exchange economy, when potential producers see that toothpaste is in high demand or running out, they quickly start producing more to meet demand, so they can *profit* from it. In a socialist nation, when incentives are gutted by heavy taxation and regulations, potential producers of toothpaste that the people want and need are likely to just throw up their hands and say, "What's the point of even *trying*?"

How and why does the free-market/voluntary-exchange (cooperation) "system" work so well for buyers and sellers? Perhaps no explanation has summed it up better than this:

> [I]n the economic system of private ownership of the means of production, the system of computation by value is necessarily employed by each independent member of society. Everybody participates...in a double way: on the one hand as a consumer and on the other as a producer. As a consumer he establishes a scale of valuation for goods ready for use in consumption. As a producer he puts goods of a higher order into such use as produces the greatest return.[37]

That is, in economies, millions of individuals make daily value judgements on goods and services. These decisions are *totally different*, because individuals vary in *millions* of ways regarding what makes them happy, what they need, and how much they're willing to pay or charge for goods and services. Think about, for example, how different *you* are from your best friend—your favorite subjects, your medical needs, your favorite foods, your tastes, and other preferences. And that's just between *two* often like-minded individuals, not among many millions of them!

Those individuals decide as best as they can what to buy (or what *not* to buy), how much of it to buy, and for what price. They also figure out what to sell (pickled beets, lumber, haircuts, computers, car repair, labor, and so on), how much of it to sell, and what to charge for it.

When central planners claim that they can take over and effectively manage this endless string of decisions made by sometimes hundreds of millions of unique individuals, those planners demonstrate one of three things:

1. **They are irrationally or cluelessly overconfident of their abilities—absolutely out of touch with reality.**

2. **They are insane, or close to it. (Maybe that's the same as #1?)**

3. **They are simply lying—entirely aware that they can't effectively make these decisions, but just hungry for power over others.**

Once again, the Bible's insistence upon respect for private property—and its teaching that the tendency of mankind to put himself first be harnessed to make life better for others—is exactly on target.

What Do You Think?

1. List some reasons why socialism fails, based on the questions for WCPs asked in this chapter. Can you think of a response a WCP might give to one of your questions to defend socialism? How could you answer that response? →

---

[37] Ludwig von Mises, *Economic Calculation in the Socialist Commonwealth* (Ludwig von Mises Institute, 1990), 15.

2. What is the basic reason why it is impossible for socialism to succeed?

3. Think of and write down an example of a government-run service, product, or department that you've encountered (or ask Mom or Dad) which could be improved by introducing a profit incentive.

5.2 – "Why the Socialist State Is Impossible"

Auberon Herbert

By 1906, when British philosopher and Parliament member Auberon Herbert (1838-1906) wrote the following essay, Karl Marx's *Communist Manifesto* had been around for 58 years, and socialism/communism had gained many academic and political supporters. In addition, Charles Darwin's *Origin of Species* had been published and had influenced readers for 47 years. That book's claim of human evolution via a mechanism of "survival of the fittest" led some elites to assume that *they* had the right—since they saw themselves as members of the "fittest"—to direct the lives of others using whatever power they obtained. And this included, of course, running economies! Auberon Herbert strongly spoke out against this abuse of power, advocating what he called *voluntaryism*: the right of persons to their own lives and property. And even though Christians wouldn't agree with all his other beliefs, Herbert did express similar views to what the Bible says are the proper functions of government. "Why the Socialist State Is Impossible" lays out a strong case for the immorality of socialism.

Why the Socialist State Is Impossible

1. Because it would presume to tell men and women how they shall employ their faculties [abilities, talents], fixing for them the nature of their work, and how much they shall receive.

2. Because it would forbid a man to work in his own fashion, and to employ his faculties for his own best advantage; and as it would be the owner of all means of production and all wealth, it would be able to compel men to accept the terms offered by the State or to starve.

3. Because, if consistently and logically carried out, it would make a State crime of buying and selling; it would allow no man to work for another, or to hire the labor of another; it would do away with private property, or reduce it to the narrowest limits; and it would fight against the natural instincts of men by systems of spying, inquisition [questioning those accused of crimes], and sharp repression.

4. Because it would consist of an enormous official class, exceeding in number and authority anything that the world has yet seen, with the workers supporting [paying their salaries via taxes] this most unnecessary multitude of privileged persons.

5. Because it would apply one universal system to all persons, good, bad, and indifferent, and would therefore be obliged to submit the good citizen to the same restrictions as were found necessary for the bad citizen.
6. Because, owing to the immense difficulty of feeding, clothing, and employing many millions of persons, and of undertaking to direct every part of their lives, the huge, complicated machinery required for such a purpose would be constantly breaking down and causing great suffering.
7. Because, when all responsibility was shifted from the individual to the State, home and family life would cease, and the State, for its own protection, would regulate marriages and the birth of children.
8. Because it could only be established by bitter fighting; and, if established, it would be destroyed by some form—such as dynamite—of the same force, which it had taught men that they might rightly employ against each other for securing their objects.
9. Because it is founded on an utterly servile [slave-like] and corrupt idea, which can bring neither happiness nor prosperity. It teaches men to give up liberty and self-guidance; to make themselves slaves of each other—under the name of the State; to consecrate the principle of universal compulsion,[38] down to the smallest details of life, in order that they may at once get a larger share of the wealth and comforts...created under the system of freedom and private enterprise...which are already beginning to pass by natural laws to those classes that hitherto [up until now] have possessed the least, and which will pass far more quickly as we better understand the value of liberty, and get rid of officialism and meddlesome politicians.

What Do You Think?

1. Fill in these: Rulers are to "remove ___ and ___, and execute ___ and ___" (Ezekiel 45:9), and "deliver the ___ out of the hand of the ___" (Jeremiah 22:3). "For rulers are not a ___ to good works, but to the ___" (Romans 13:3-4), and they are "sent by him for the ___ of ___" (1 Peter 2:14).
2. How do the limits placed on government in those above verses line up with Herbert's above essay?
3. Briefly, in writing, sum up two of Herbert's points (except for the last one).
4. What is the main idea expressed in Herbert's last point?

5.3 – The Broken Window

These two short selections are taken from an 1850 essay titled "That Which Is Seen, and That Which Is Not Seen," by Frenchman Frederic Bastiat, one of the greatest political and economic writers of all time. Remember what Henry Hazlitt identified as the two main mistakes of bad

---

[38] To "consecrate the principle of universal compulsion": means to make sacred and unquestionable the idea of government control of everyone's lives.

economists? The first is looking at an economic policy's effects upon just one group, instead of all groups. The second is looking at an economic policy's effects for just the short term, instead of the long term. Hazlitt was an enthusiastic admirer of Bastiat, and built upon his ideas in his own economic writings. You'll enjoy both of these short essays, which teach economic principles in a lively, forceful style, using one of the most famous examples in all of economics: the case of the broken window.

Introduction

In the department of economy, an act, a habit, an institution, a law, gives birth not only to an effect, but to a *series* of effects. Of these effects, the first only is immediate; it manifests itself simultaneously with its cause—*it is seen*. The others unfold in succession—*they are not seen*: it is well for us if they are *foreseen*. Between a good and a bad economist this constitutes the whole difference—the one takes account of the *visible* effect; the other takes account both of the effects which are *seen* and also of those which it is necessary to *foresee*. Now this difference is enormous, for it almost always happens that when the immediate consequence is favorable, the ultimate consequences are fatal, *and the converse*. Hence it follows that the bad economist pursues a small present good, which will be followed by a great evil to come, while the true economist pursues a great good to come, at the risk of a small present evil.

In fact, it is the same in the science of health, arts, and in that of morals. It often happens, that the sweeter the first fruit of a habit is, the more bitter are the consequences. Take, for example, immorality, idleness, prodigality [excessive spending of money]. When, therefore, a man, absorbed in the effect which *is seen*, has not yet learned to discern those which are *not* seen, he gives way to fatal habits, not only by inclination, but by calculation.

This explains the fatally grievous condition of mankind. Ignorance surrounds its cradle: then its actions are determined by their first consequences, the only ones which, in its first stage, it can see. It is only in the long run that it learns to take account of the others. It has to learn this lesson from two very different masters—experience and foresight. Experience teaches effectually, but brutally. It makes us acquainted with all the effects of an action, by causing us to feel them; and we cannot fail to finish by knowing that fire burns, if we have burned ourselves. For this rough teacher, I should like, if possible, to substitute a more gentle one. I mean Foresight. For this purpose I shall examine the consequences of certain economical phenomena, by placing in opposition to each other those *which are seen*, and those *which are not seen*.

The Broken Window

Have you ever witnessed the anger of the good shopkeeper, Jacques Bonhomme,[39] when his careless son happened to break a pane of glass? If you have

---

[39] The name "Jacques Bonhomme" means "Jack Goodfellow" in English—in other words, just an average guy.

been present at such a scene, you will most assuredly bear witness to the fact, that every one of the spectators, were there even thirty of them, by common consent apparently, offered the unfortunate owner this invariable consolation: "It is an ill wind that blows nobody good. Everybody must live, and what would become of the glaziers [glass cutters] if panes of glass were never bro-ken?"

Frederic Bastiat

Now, this form of sympathy contains an entire theory, which it will be well to show up in this simple case, seeing that it is precisely the same as that which, unhappily, regulates the greater part of our economic institutions.

Suppose it cost six francs to repair the damage, and you say that the accident brings six francs to the glazier's trade—that it encourages that trade to the amount of six francs—I grant it; I have not a word to say against it; you reason justly. The glazier comes, performs his task, receives his six francs, rubs his hands, and, in his heart, blesses the careless child. All this is *that which is seen*.

But if, on the other hand, you come to the conclusion, as is too often the case, that it is a good thing to break windows, that it causes money to circulate, and that the encouragement of industry in general will be the result of it, you will oblige me to call out, "Stop there! Your theory is confined to that *which is seen*; it takes no account of that *which is not seen*."

It is not seen that as our shopkeeper has spent six francs upon one thing, he cannot spend them upon another. *It is not seen* that if he had not had a window to replace, he would, perhaps, have replaced his old shoes, or added another book to his library. In short, he would have employed his six francs in some way which this accident has prevented.

Let us take a view of industry in general, as affected by this circumstance. The window being broken, the glazier's trade is encouraged to the amount of six francs: *this is that which is seen*.

If the window had not been broken, the shoemaker's trade (or some other) would have been encouraged to the amount of six francs: this is *that which is not seen*.

And if *that which is not seen* is taken into consideration, because it is a negative fact, as well as that which is seen, because it is a positive fact, it will be understood that neither industry *in general*, nor the sum total of *national labor*, is affected, whether windows are broken or not.

Now let us consider Jacques B. himself. In the former supposition, that of the window being broken, he spends six francs, and has neither more nor less than he had before, the enjoyment of a window.

In the second, where we suppose the window not to have been broken, he would have spent six francs in shoes, and would have had at the same time the enjoyment of a pair of shoes *and* of a window.

Now, as Jacques B. forms a part of society, we must come to the conclusion, that, taking it altogether, and making an estimate of its enjoyments and its labors, *it has lost the value of the broken window*.

Whence we arrive at this unexpected conclusion: "Society loses the value of things which are uselessly destroyed"; and we must agree to a saying which will make the hair of protectionists[40] stand on end—to break, to spoil, to waste, is not to encourage national labor; or, more briefly, "destruction is not profit."

What will you say, *Moniteur Industriel*[41]—what will you say, disciples of good Mr. Chamans, who has calculated with so much precision how much trade would gain by the burning of Paris, from the number of houses it would be necessary to rebuild?[42]

I am sorry to disturb these ingenious calculations, as far as their spirit has been introduced into our legislation; but I beg him to begin them again, by taking into the account *that which is not seen*, and placing it alongside of *that which is seen*.

The reader must take care to remember that there are not two persons only, but three concerned in the little scene which I have submitted to his attention. One of them, Jacques B., represents the consumer, reduced, by an act of destruction, to one enjoyment instead of two. Another, under the title of the glazier, shows us the producer, whose trade is encouraged by the accident. The third is the shoemaker (or some other tradesman), whose labor suffers proportionably by the same cause. It is this third person who is always kept in the shade, and who, personating *that which is not seen*, is a necessary element of the problem. It is he who shows us how absurd it is to think we see a profit in an act of destruction. It is he who will soon teach us that it is not less absurd to see a profit in a restriction [governments limiting what some industries may produce], which is, after all, nothing else than a partial destruction. Therefore, if you will only go to the root of all the arguments which are offered in its favor, all you will find will be the paraphrase of this vulgar [common, unsophisticated] saying—*What would become of the glaziers, if nobody ever broke windows*?

What Do You Think?

1. What does Bastiat say is nearly always true when an economic policy looks good immediately? What does he compare this to?
2. Sum up the case of the broken window: what the short-sighted person claims, and how Bastiat corrects this claim.

---

[40] Protectionists believe that a government should *protect* their industry, often with taxes placed upon foreign producers of that same good or service.
[41] *Le Moniteur Industriel*, a French publication that supported government protection
[42] Bastiat here refers to Saint-Chamans, a government official who argued in an essay that the Great London Fire of 1666 was a *benefit* to England.

5.4 – The Broken-Window Fallacy and War • Quiz 4

Yesterday we read Frederic Bastiat's parable of the broken window. Keeping his example in mind, and applying it to other scenarios, is one way we can think more clearly about economic policies. The "broken-window fallacy," as this concept is often called, helps us remember that destroying property hurts an economy. But at this point you might very reasonably think this: *Isn't that obvious? How could anybody believe that **destroying** things helps make an economy more prosperous?*

That's understandable, absolutely! But bad economists—and disingenuous economists—have used forms of the broken-window fallacy to make excuses for misguided and awful government economic policies for centuries. And frankly, in our day, we are *surrounded* by "experts," TV news "talking heads," educators, and government officials who, right to our faces, tell us things that defy all human experience, logic, and common sense:

- *"There are dozens of different genders—probably many more."*
- *"Warmer summers occur because of man-made climate change."*
- *"Burning down buildings and killing others who have harmed no one is 'mostly peaceful.'"*
- *"Colder winters occur because of man-made climate change."*
- *"Face masks with holes that are far too large to ever stop viral particles from passing through... will—we are **positive**—stop viral particles from passing through."*
- *"Warmer winters occur because of man-made climate change."*

Politician Stacey Abrams, Not Worried a Bit About the Deadliest Virus in the History of the Universe
PHOTO: Twitter/@staceyabrams

- *"You need to wear a mask to protect yourself and others from the deadliest virus in history...but I don't need to—I work for the **government**!"*
- *"Cooler summers occur because of man-made climate change."*
- *"Men can be women if they want to be. In fact, men can even give **birth**!"*
- *"It's important that we shut down churches to fight this 'pandemic,' but it's also important that liquor bars and gambling joints stay open."*

- *"The word **woman** can't be exactly defined."*

And so on. The point is this: **By this time we should be used to government-influenced and government-paid experts regularly telling us bizarre, obviously untrue, and/or irrational things, including the notion that destroying property and other wealth "benefits the economy."**

In fact, as an example, some politicians and economists have even argued that *war itself* is good for the economy! That is, they say, in a nutshell, this:

> Well, yes, it's true—we *did* bomb entire cities during the war, and... you know, if you want to get *picky* about it, sure, I guess we did kill thousands of innocent people, or whatever...but that's actually a *positive*! Those bombed-out cities will provide *jobs* for all kinds of construction workers, bricklayers, concrete manufacturers, electricians, and...uh, doctors and funeral directors, I guess. And yes, we did raise taxes on everybody to pay for the soldiers' salaries, food, guns, helmets, bullets, boots, bombs, and planes. *But* those soldiers spent their salaries on groceries and clothes and other items, and that spending *really helped the economy*! And the money that the bomb and gun and tank manufacturers made was put back into the economy, too!

I'm sure you're able to see that this ridiculous claim is a just a horrific version of Bastiat's "that which is seen, and that which is *not* seen" concept. It's a hideous myth that's been debunked repeatedly for eons. In fact, Scottish political writer James Mill addressed the ridiculous idea that "war is a benefit" over 200 years ago in his 1808 work *Commerce Defended*:

> A thousand ploughmen consume fully as much corn and cloth in...a year as a regiment of soldiers. But the difference between the kinds of consumption is immense. The labor of the ploughman has, during the year, served to call into existence a quantity of property, which not only repays the corn and cloth which he has consumed, but repays it with a profit. The soldier, on the other hand, produces nothing.
>
> What he has consumed is gone...its place is left absolutely vacant. The country is the poorer for his consumption, to the full amount of what he has consumed. It is not the poorer, but the richer for what the ploughman has consumed, because, during the time he was consuming it, he has reproduced what does more than replace it.[43]

What Do You Think?

1. Explain in your own words the main point that James Mill makes in the excerpt at the chapter's end.
2. Explain how the broken-window fallacy would apply to these claims: →

---

[43] James Mill, *Commerce Defended: An Answer to the Arguments by which Mr. Spence, Mr. Cobbett, and Others, Have Attempted to Prove That Commerce Is Not a Source of National Wealth*, 1808, Online Library of Liberty, https://oll.libertyfund.org/title/mill-commerce-defended-1808.

- "It's actually good for the economy that you broke your leg, Mom; you helped to provide work for that doctor and nurse."
- "I know the hurricane blew all those houses down, but it's been an overall positive, since it provided jobs for construction workers."

 Take Quiz 4 (online or in-person students only). Feel free to use your notes, but there is a time limit!

6.1 – Test 2

If you're in my in-person or online Economics class, take Test 2 today. This test focuses on material from Weeks 4-5, but also might contain material from previous weeks. Review your notes, then take Test 2!

6.2 – "Inflation in One Page"

Have you ever wondered what *inflation* is, but thought it would be too hard to understand? Well, you're in luck—in a few minutes, you'll get it! This short essay, "Inflation in One Page," was written in 1978 by Henry Hazlitt, when he was in his eighties.[44] The paragraph directly below is Hazlitt's original introduction on his piece, and this beautiful little essay comes courtesy of the Foundation for Economic Education. I strongly recommend that you read this short essay **twice**; you'll understand it much better the second time through, and the review questions will be much easier to answer.

• • • • •

A correspondent, heading a group of "Inflation Fighters," recently sent me a one-page typewritten summary of their case against inflation, and asked for my opinion of it. The statement was sincere and well-intentioned, but as with the great bulk of what is being written about inflation, it was confused in both its analysis and its recommendations. I wrote approving his effort to "do something," and approving also his idea of trying to state the cause and cure for inflation on a single page, but suggested the following substitute statement.

1. Inflation is an increase in the quantity of money and credit. Its chief consequence is soaring prices. Therefore inflation—if we misuse the term to mean the rising prices themselves—is caused solely by printing more money. For this the government's monetary policies are entirely responsible.

---

[44] Because of the font size in and layout of this book, it's a little more than one page!

2. The most frequent reason for printing more money is the existence of an unbalanced budget. Unbalanced budgets are caused by extravagant expenditures which the government is unwilling or unable to pay for by raising corresponding tax revenues. The excessive expenditures are mainly the result of government efforts to redistribute wealth and income—in short, to force the productive to support the unproductive. This erodes the working incentives of both the productive and the unproductive.

3. The causes of inflation are not, as so often said, "multiple and complex," but simply the result of printing too much money. There is no such thing as "cost-push" inflation. If, without an increase in the stock of money, wage or other costs are forced up, and producers try to pass these costs along by raising their selling prices, most of them will merely sell fewer goods. The result will be reduced output and loss of jobs. Higher costs can only be passed along in higher selling prices when consumers have more money to pay the higher prices.

4. Price controls[45] cannot stop or slow down inflation. They always do harm. Price controls simply squeeze or wipe out profit margins, disrupt production, and lead to bottlenecks [surpluses of unsold items] and shortages. All government price and wage control, or even "monitoring," is merely an attempt by the politicians to shift the blame for inflation on to producers and sellers instead of their own monetary policies.

5. Prolonged inflation never "stimulates" the economy. On the contrary, it unbalances, disrupts, and misdirects production and employment. Unemployment is mainly caused by excessive wage rates in some industries, brought about either by extortionate [unreasonable] union demands, by minimum wage laws (which keep teenagers and the unskilled out of jobs), or by prolonged and overgenerous unemployment insurance [which pays those who are not working].

6. To avoid irreparable damage, the budget must be balanced at the earliest possible moment, and not in some sweet by-and-by. Balance must be brought about by slashing reckless spending, and not by increasing a tax burden that is already undermining incentives and production.

(Now go back and read those six points a second time!)

• • • • •

To finish up for today, watch "Why Not Just Print More Money?", a three-minute video produced by the Foundation for Economic Education. *Take notes on it, and bring these to class next week!* You can access the video by taking a picture of the QR code to the right with your smart phone, or by searching YouTube for the video using the title name above. **(Don't forget to answer the review questions on the next page!)**

---

[45] Price controls are government orders that say, for example, "Your bread-baking business may not charge more than $5 per loaf."

What Do You Think?

1. Define *inflation*. What is the common "misuse" of the term?
2. Why does government prefer printing money to increasing taxes?
3. How does the answer to #2 "erode the working incentives of both the productive and the unproductive"?
4. What does Hazlitt say needs to happen to "avoid irreparable damage"?

6.3 – Inflation: Counterfeiting and Robbery

Baseball Cards and the Angel Gabriel

Governments obtain money in three ways: taxing, borrowing it, or inflating (creating it out of thin air). As Henry Hazlitt pointed out in yesterday's reading, governments prefer to inflate, since they like to spend more of other people's money with-out having to be accountable for their actions. Because *voters*—at least the ones who are not insane—don't like higher taxes, and politicians who raise taxes to pay for increased government spending can face hordes of angry voters.

Inflation is not a mysterious process which only a few Chosen Ones can understand; it refers to nothing more than the government's creating more money, which makes the value of existing money less.[46] If you had a rare baseball card, for example, that was worth $1 million, because it was the only one known to exist, what would happen to the value of your card if someone found 10 more of the same card in his grandmother's attic?

Obviously, the value of your card would decrease. And what would happen if 100 of those cards were found? Exactly!

Historian Murray Rothbard used a helpful illustration to explain inflation. He described a scenario in which the angel Gabriel comes down from heaven one evening and doubles everyone's money. What would happen in the morning? Everyone at first would be overjoyed: "I'm rich!" Next, what would everyone do with the money? Many would spend it, of course! Those who rushed out to spend the new money *be-fore anyone else did* would be wildly successful at buying all kinds of items. But when others began coming in waves to spend their money, sellers would adjust their prices. *Up.*

And up again.

And then: up.

Then they'd raise their prices again.

Next, they would increase them.

Then...you get the picture.

---

[46] Today inflation includes the use of computers to "create" money.

If you were one of the unfortunate ones who woke up last or started to spend your new money last, it wouldn't be worth much. Even worse, stores everywhere that you normally shopped at would have raised their prices—some drastically, based on how much increased demand there was for their products. Your extra money would now be worth much less, and the value of the money you already had now would be worth less than it was.[47]

Likewise, when a government creates new money, those groups who receive it *first* get the full value of it; everyone else's prices rise as the new money works its way through the economy. Three questions, then, we ought to ask and answer about this process.

First, when a government inflates the supply of money, does it evenly spread out the "new money" to everyone? No, it doesn't. (I'm obviously not in favor of inflation, but if a government *did* do that, wouldn't that be the *fair* way to do it?)

Second, which groups get the money first? The answer: those whom the government wants to pay off, and privileged groups closely connected to government—banks, billion-dollar corporations, military equipment manufacturers, and so on.

Third, what group is hurt *worst* by inflation? (Think about it for a minute.) If you said, "The poor," you're correct. Inflation hurts the poor in two ways: (1) They're often at the "end" of the money chain and receive it last; and (2) when the price of a loaf of bread or clothing or electricity increases, it hurts the poor much more than it does a millionaire, since the poor are less able to overcome price increases. (For example, if bread were to rise to $20 per loaf, the poor would be much more harshly affected than millionaires would be.) God despises plundering the poor to benefit the rich:

> *He that oppresseth the poor to increase his riches, and he that giveth to the rich, shall surely come to want (Proverbs 22:16).*

"Greedy Business Owners" and Coin Clipping

One of the worst characteristics of inflation is that almost everyone misunderstands it. **Remember: The true definition of inflation is not "higher prices."** As pointed out in yesterday's reading, inflation is defined as "an increase in the quantity of money and credit." When the government inflates the money supply, grocery store, gas station, and restaurant owners raise their prices because they recognize, like the baseball card example, that the value of each unit of money is worth less. But when this happens, unfortunately, many individuals tend to believe something like this:

> *Those greedy store owners are raising their prices again!*

Of course, this is nonsense; did all business owners get greedy at the same time? What we know about mankind's nature tells us that business owners, unless influenced by unusual circumstances, *always* want to sell their goods for

---

[47] Murray Rothbard, *The Mystery of Banking* (Ludwig von Mises Institute, 2008), 45-47.

as high a price as possible. But they can't just go around raising their prices any time they feel like it; they know very well that this will de-crease the number of their buyers, since—again, because of man's nature—buyers always want to *buy* goods for as *low* a price as possible!

When governments inflate, the currency, business owners realize that the money they receive for their goods is worth less, so it takes more of that money to equal the old price—thus, higher prices, a *result* of inflation.

Before the advent of the printing press and computers, corrupt government officials would follow an inflationary process of **debasement** of currency—lowering its value. An ancient Roman ruler, for example, might take existing silver and gold coins from the people, melt them down, and then produce and distribute new coins that were smaller and/or contained less gold or silver than they did previously—*because that ruler stole some of the gold and silver from the old coins for himself.* When the people realized what had happened, they knew each coin was worth less, and business owners increased their prices to reflect the fact that the new coins individually were worth less than the old ones.

A form of this debasement happened in the U. S. as well. Up until 1965, American silver dollars, half-dollars, quarters, dimes, and nickels included *some* silver, so they were inherently valuable. But in 1965, the U. S. Government debased the currency by removing all the silver from newly-minted coins. (Coin collectors even today still hunt for and save coins made before 1965.)

What Is <u>Real</u> Wealth?

Earlier, we briefly discussed the idea that maybe government should go ahead and inflate, but spread the money out *evenly* and fairly. Then we'd *all* be richer!

But wait—would we? What *is* real wealth, after all? Recall that earlier in this book (see Section 3.4) we read that the Bible described Abram as *"very rich in cattle, in silver, and in gold."* Why were those items considered wealth? We could ask a similar question today: What do the rich have today that makes them rich? Is it pieces of green rectangular paper?

No, obviously not. Although we could certainly still say, even today, that anyone who owns a great deal of cattle, silver, and gold is rich, most wealth today comes in different forms like homes, computers, cars, airplanes, land, swimming pools, clothing, chicken sandwiches with two pickles on them, and so on. What if the government gave everybody $1000—for that matter, why not give everybody $100,000, or even $1 billion? Would you instantly see more buildings, cars, homes, clothes, computers, hospitals, air conditioners, and jars of delicious pickled beets magically appear out of thin air? Would any new real *wealth* have been created?

No, of course not. Giving out "money" to everyone does absolutely nothing to increase *real* wealth. It *does*, however, make *some* wealthier when governments inflate—again, those privileged persons at the top of the chain who receive the new money first and trade it for *real* items of wealth.

Inflation is plunder, and it's unjust. It also violates what the Bible says is government's true, moral purpose. And we can dismiss the ridiculous claim of any politician who claims to want to make the people wealthier by inflating the money supply. If government officials *really* wanted to make everyone wealthier, they would stop taxing and regulating businesses, allowing them to invest in technology and machines that make goods cheaper. This would make it easier for families—especially poor families—to afford more products using the money they make now.

What Do You Think?

1. Make sure you understand the baseball card/Angel Gabriel scenarios.
2. When governments inflate, who gets the money first? How does inflation especially hurt the poor?
3. Explain what is wrong with this claim: "Businesses are raising their prices again. That's because they're greedy!"
4. Why would handing out $100 million to every U.S. family not make them all instantly wealthier?
5. Imagine you have $10,000 saved up to buy your first car, and the government inflates the money supply. What happens to your savings if you leave it in the bank? How does inflation affect those who have saved for retirement?

6.4 – The Federal Reserve: Stealing 97 Percent (So Far)

As Seen in *The Communist Manifesto*!

In *The Communist Manifesto*, author Karl Marx lays out 10 steps a ruler (or group of rulers) should take to turn a nation into a communist state. The steps include abolishing private property, putting the government in charge of all transportation and communication, taxing individual incomes, creating a system of government-run schools for children, and so on. Here's the fifth step:

> Centralization of Credit in the Hands of the State, by Means of a National Bank with State Capital and an Exclusive Monopoly.

In 1913 the U. S. Congress executed this step by creating the Federal Reserve, also known as the "Fed."[48] We're not going to dive deeply into the Fed's inner workings—just a few facts on and an analysis of its morality and effectiveness. The Fed is nothing more than a government agency that *resembles* a bank, and it prints money—that is, it *inflates* the money supply—to pay for immoral, plundering, and/or excessive government spending. It can't go bankrupt like a *real* bank, since it has the power to print all the money it wants. We've seen what inflation does to the value of money. What you might not know is that since its inception in 1913, the Fed has devalued the dollar about 97 percent. In other words, a dollar today is only worth about three percent of what it was worth when the Fed came into existence—that is, items cost roughly 33 times more than they did in 1913!

Before 1913, Americans often used gold and silver coins for money, and to a lesser extent afterwards, at least until 1965, when the government started minting coins with zero silver content. The word **dollar** has historically referred to a specific *weight* of gold—usually some fraction of an ounce, such as 1/20th. Paper money in the U. S. was just a receipt, or certificate, that you could "cash in" for gold or silver. In fact, U. S. dollar bills, like the one below, read "SILVER CERTIFICATE" on the top, and "ONE DOLLAR IN SILVER PAYABLE TO THE BEARER ON DEMAND" on the bottom. This meant that the holder of that dollar bill could redeem it for the equivalent amount of silver at any time. (Most didn't, since paper money was more convenient to carry, and they believed they could redeem it at any time they wanted.) Now, dollar bills say "FEDERAL RESERVE NOTE" at the top, and there is no silver or gold backing all these paper dollars.

A 1935 Silver Certificate Dollar Bill
Photo courtesy of the National Numismatic Collection, NMAH, Smithsonian Institution

The "Founding Fathers" on Inflation

Inflation is used by the powerful to enrich themselves by stealing from the middle class and the poor. Many early American statesmen—Alexander Hamilton

---

[48] It also implemented Marx's step of an income tax by passing the Sixteenth Amendment in the same year.

was one exception—spoke out on the dangers of giving banks and governments the ability to manipulate the economy with paper money:

> **John Adams:** All the perplexities, confusions, and distress in America arise not from defects in their Constitution or Confederation, not from a want [lack] of honor or virtue, so much as from downright ignorance of the nature of coin, credit, and circulation.
>
> **Thomas Jefferson:** Paper is poverty...it is only the ghost of money, and not money itself.
>
> **Andrew Jackson:** Expansion of the money supply through spurious [counterfeit] paper currency is always attended [accompanied] by a loss to the laboring classes.
>
> **Daniel Webster:** [O]f all the contrivances [devices] for cheating the laboring classes of mankind, none has been found more effectual than that which deludes them with paper money.

To sum up those ideas: Ignorance about how money causes many problems, and the creation of paper money—which any person *outside* of government would be arrested for doing—cheats the middle class and the poor.

Interest in a Free Economy

Along with inflating the money supply, the Fed also manipulates an economy by raising and lowering interest rates. **Interest** is simply a special name for the cost of borrowing money. If you borrow $10,000, for example, and the lending bank charges you eight percent interest, you must pay back that $10,000, plus eight percent of $10,000 ($800) on top of that $10,000, which is called the **principal**.

But the government has no business deciding what the cost of borrowing money will be any more than it has deciding what the cost of shoes or oranges should be! In a free economy, borrowers should be free to decide on what percent of interest they're willing to pay, and lenders should be free to decide on what percent they want to charge.

Here's a basic economics question for you: What factors contribute to-ward the price of a product—for example, oranges?

Your answer no doubt will include factors such as the amount of oranges available, as well as the willingness of consumers to buy them. In other words, *supply and demand*.

Well, if it works for buying and selling oranges, it works for borrowing and lending money, too! Here's what happens to interest rates in a *free* economy, and how it benefits participants:

- **In a free-trade economy, lenders and borrowers charge and pay any interest rate they want**, exactly like they charge and pay any price for any other good or service they want.
- **If individuals save more of their money, that means there is more available to lend, and the price to borrow it decreases.** Just like any-

thing else, *when the supply of something increases, its price decreases.* If more money is available to lend, then, the price of borrowing that money—again, this is called **interest**—decreases. *Now more business owners can afford to borrow money.*

- **If the amount of savings decreases, that means there is less money to lend, and interest rates *increase*.** Some businesses then decide to wait on borrowing money. Also, when interest rates increase, more saving occurs, so eventually as the amount of money saved goes back up, the cost of borrowing money decreases again.
- **More saving means more money to borrow**, so more businesses can invest in new inventions, technologies, and machines that reduce the cost of producing items like shirts and computers and bread. Since these products are cheaper to produce, the prices of those products decrease. *That increases the value of the money in your pocket, since it can now buy more goods and services than it could before.*

To restate how interest is determined in a voluntary-exchange economy:

1. When savings *increase*, the price of borrowing money *decreases*, since there is more of it available to borrow—just like the price of anything else decreases when the supply of it increases. Therefore, *when individuals save more, business owners can more easily afford to borrow money* to expand their businesses, invest in new technology and machines, and so on.
2. When savings *decrease*, the price of borrowing money *increases*, since there is less of it available to borrow. In that case, more businesses (though not all!) hold off on borrowing, waiting for the price to decrease.
3. When individuals realize that interest rates are higher, they tend to save more money (to earn more from interest paid), so that drives the amount of savings up, and then...the cost of borrowing money *decreases* again!
4. Just like the price of any other item on earth that's bought and sold, the price of borrowing money in a free economy *regulates itself.*

Let's Ask the Same Question Again....

When the Fed controls interest rates and inflates the currency supply, it warps a freely functioning economy that operates on the choices that tens or hundreds of millions of individuals—buyers and sellers—make every day in their own self-interest. Instead, this Fed interference sends wrong signals to business owners about borrowing and lending, causing mistakes in their business decisions. When business owners must take measures like laying off employees or closing shops to correct their flawed decisions based on distorted government economic policies, slumps in the economy occur. These slumps are known as **recessions**, and if they worsen and stay worse for longer, they're called **depressions**.[49] Austrian economists (those economists in favor of free markets, remember) have long believed that *central banks, which inflate or manipulate interest rates, are the main cause of these economic downturns*:

> Recessions or depressions are due to the...policy of inflation. They reveal the mistakes and malinvestments businesses made under the influence of the inflation. Thus recessions or depressions are periods of correction in which business people try to better adjust production and prices to what consumers want.[50]

Beginning less than a decade after its creation, from July 1921 to July 1929, the Federal Reserve inflated the money supply in the United States from $45 billion to $73 billion, an increase of about 62 percent.[51] The result: a stock market crash three months later, in October 1929, the month commonly credited as the beginning of America's Great Depression.

• • • • •

It's completely reasonable and fair to ask the same question to those planners who want to decide what interest rates should be that we asked those planners who think they have the right (not to mention the ability) to decide how many oranges, shoes, toothbrushes, and other items that should be produced in an economy. That is, millions of buyers and sellers in an economy make personal decisions every day about oranges (to take just one item)—how many to buy, how many to grow, how much they're willing to pay for them, and at what price they're willing to sell them. And so we could rightfully ask the central planners these questions:

> What makes you think that *you* have some mysterious, specialized knowledge—not to mention the moral *right*—to *command* to orange sellers how many oranges they ought to grow, and how much they should charge for them? The millions of orange buyers in this country already *do* that!
>
> Do you really think that you and your group of planners know better than *they* do? Shouldn't you defer to the wishes of those millions of buyers and sellers? If you don't think you should, where's your *proof* that you know better than everyone else, and that everyone involved should bow to your demands?

(At this point, you might want to visualize calm, soothing waves lapping up on the shore, so you don't get too worked up and tempted to find a central planner somewhere and punch him in the nose.)

---

[49] We look more closely at America's Great Depression in *American Government for Christian Homeschoolers*.
[50] Richard Maybury, *Whatever Happened to Penny Candy?* (Bluestocking Press, 2015), 56.
[51] Murray Rothbard, *America's Great Depression* (Murray N. Rothbard, 1963), 91-93.

And similar questions should be raised to those who think they have the right and ability to determine interest rates:

> What makes you think *you* know better—and should have the *right*—to decide what price or percentage rate the cost of borrowing money should be? Do you know better than the cumulative decisions of tens of millions of borrowers and lenders?

What Do You Think?

1. Why do you think Karl Marx included a national bank in his blueprint to turn nations into communist states?
2. Define *interest*. Why should a government <u>not</u> be involved in interest rates any more than it should be involved in the price of cars or potatoes?
3. How does the amount of savings in a free economy affect interest rates?
4. What do Austrian economists believe that national banks' manipulating interest rates causes?

7.1 – CLAIM: "The Government Needs to Help Doctors!"

From memory if possible, fill in the blanks of the below four verses, which lay out the proper, Biblical roles of governments:

- To *"[R]emove ___ and ___, and execute ___ and ___"* (Ezekiel 45:9)
- To *"Deliver the ___ out of the hand of the oppressor"* (Jeremiah 22:3)
- To punish *"___"* (1 Peter 2:13-14)
- To be a *"terror"* and *"revenger"* to *"___"* (Romans 13:4)

• • • • •

The Scenario: Imagine you're in a college economics class, and another student in your class makes this claim:

> I think that the government should provide *free* schooling and other training for doctors and nurses. We *need* more of them in America, because health care is important—I mean, just look at all the sick people we have in this country!

How could you respond to this claim, based on what you've learned about economics so far? Write a short summary of your response, and if you're in my in-person or online class, bring it to our next class.

7.2 – Prices, Price Controls, and "Price Gouging"

The Miracle of Prices

Why do some stores have discount bins at the front? We've all seen them: a pile of apparently random items tossed into a giant container, marked down—sometimes drastically.

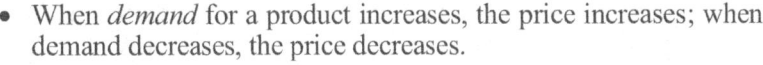

The reason for those bins is easy: The seller of those discount items is reacting to signals by adjusting pricing. That is, the items have sat in the store for weeks or months without selling, so...it's time to mark them down!

Let's briefly sum up what we've learned so far about prices:

- When *demand* for a product increases, the price increases; when demand decreases, the price decreases.

- When the *supply* of a product increases, the price decreases; when the supply of that product decreases, the price increases.

- When it's clear that a product is in high demand and commands a high price, others get into that business and produce that item; this creates competition and drives the price down for consumers.

- When governments inflate the money supply, prices increase, since the value of that money decreases.

- In a free economy, buyers and sellers determine prices by a nearly uncountable number of individual decisions. Buyers constantly adjust their willingness to pay certain prices based on supply and demand; sellers constantly adjust their prices based on the same.

To restate: In a free economy, prices determine the decisions that producers of goods and services make—what to produce, and how much to produce. The price "system" is an absolute miracle. It's not even something that's comprehensible; the human mind simply cannot grasp the countless number of price adjustments that occur every day, based on what buyers are willing to pay for items, and how much sellers can charge for them.

This is partly how a free market regulates itself.

Business owners by the millions in a nation are constantly trying to stay in business and make money by making sure their customers are happy—*businesses driven by the wants and needs of those who are often total strangers!* And hundreds of millions of consumers make daily value judgements based on price and other factors. No group of planners on earth, no matter how smart they think they are, could possibly hope to replicate it.

But that doesn't mean they don't *try*, of course.

The Absurdity of Price Controls

When a government meddles in the economy, distortions and business miscalculations occur; these meddlings can cause higher prices. (This is exactly what inflation does, of course.) On occasion, government officials decide that they're going to *do* something about those high prices on certain items, so they set **price controls**. (This is sometimes called "price fixing.") A government official makes an announcement that sounds something like this:

> The price of gasoline has skyrocketed recently—but we're *sure* it has nothing at all to do with any of *our* polices, of course; it's probably just those greedy gas station owners. Since gas has become much more expensive, to make it more affordable, we're making it *illegal* for gas stations to charge more than $5 per gallon.

Before we address the insanity and immorality of that statement, let's list four reasons why governments should never impose price controls:

1. Meddling in pricing, 99.999999999999372 percent of the time, has absolutely nothing to do with the legitimate, moral functions of government as taught by God's Word.

2. Even the smartest group of government planners in the history of the world could never even come close to setting prices as accurately and quickly as millions of buyers and sellers. (It's possible I might have mentioned this before.)

3. Using the gasoline price example above, government planners who set price controls on gas make one of Henry Hazlitt's two basic "bad economist" mistakes: looking at the effects of their policy on only *one* group: gas buyers—although "gas buyers" is a large group.

4. The gasoline that is the property of the gas station owners is—follow me closely here—*gasoline that is the property of the gas station owners.* That gasoline is *their* private property. They *bought* it, they *own* it, and they have the right to charge *whatever price they want* for it. What moral right does a government have to tell business owners what they may or may not do—assuming those business owners are not violating the rights of others—*with their own property*?

Go back a few pages and read the third bullet point on what we've learned about prices. Do you understand what it's saying? To summarize: When an item's price goes up, and producers are making good profits selling it, *others try to get in the game and make profits too.*

Now, what do you think happens to the number of producers of a good or service when the price of that item *may not* go up because the government *forbids* it?

You guessed it! When that happens, nobody *else* wants to jump in and produce more of it. In fact, *some current producers of that product—if not many or most—will even quit producing it!* So the state, which institutes price controls on a good or service to make it *more* available to buyers...makes it *less* available to them. Brilliant.

What About "Price Gouging"?

Whenever a hurricane or other natural disaster threatens an area, residents rush to buy flashlights, bottled water, batteries, gasoline, and other items they might need more if they're hit by the hurricane, or just if they lose power. When sellers of these items realize there's a higher demand for them, they naturally raise prices, and the familiar cry arises: "*Price gouging!* Those stores are *price gouging*!" But here are a few questions sensible persons should ask about that claim:

Question 1: What is the *exact* definition of "price gouging"? That is, how does the government know the *exact* price at which an item morphs from being just expensive into something affected by "price gouging"? Do government officials have a book of "price gouging" points that an angel tosses down from heaven or something? If those officials say they *do* have a book like this, does it include every item in the entire nation being sold? And if so, does this book make a big dent in the ground when it lands?

Question 2: Whose property is it? Don't "price gougers" *own* what they are selling to consumers? Don't they have the right to charge whatever they want for it?

Question 3: What happens to the number of producers of an item when they're not allowed to sell it above a certain price? We already know the answer to that question.

Question 4: What happens to buyers and sellers of a product that has been "price gouged"? When an item's cost increases, buyers, of course, buy it less. But other buyers who *really* want or need that item will certainly still be willing to buy it. For example, if, during a hurricane, the price of gas doubles, buyers who really don't need gas will tend to hold off buying it until the price falls. Others who *really* need it—to, say, run a generator to keep the heat on for a sick grandmother—will no doubt pay the (temporarily) higher price.

Now, what do you think would have happened to the *supply* of gas during the hurricane if the government had tried to prohibit or punish so-called "price gouging"?

No doubt you realize that if that happened, *more consumers would have tried to buy gasoline*—even for less important things, like running their generators so they could watch TV. In fact, a law forbidding so-called "price gouging" on gasoline would have also led consumers to buy even *more* gas than they really needed, and it's less likely, as a result, that those families who *really* needed the gas for critical uses would have been able to get it. Do we really want those who really *need* a product to be able to get it? If we do, allowing the raising of prices—*which reduces the number of buyers*—is one way to keep that product available to them.

Let's put it this way: If gas stations were forced to keep their prices the same in the face of a hurricane, what would happen to the amount of gas that the average customer bought? It's obvious: Gas customers would line up at every gas station in sight, and most of them, if not nearly *all* of them, would completely fill up their cars. Some of them might even bring gas cans to fill up, too. And who would lose out?

The people at the back of the lines! They're more likely to get less, little, or no gas. In fact, it might be that the elderly—those who might have a harder time without a generator filled with gasoline *and* might take longer getting to a gas station—would be harder hit. Is *that* the government's answer, then, to solving the issue of gas availability? Rewarding those who get in line first, and leaving behind later arrivers? *That's* supposed to be "fair"!?

Question 5: Is anybody *forcing* others to buy a product for a certain price? The truthful answer to that question is "No." Consumers can choose any time they want *not* to pay the price that a seller charges if they think it's too high, or otherwise not worth the product or service. Since this is true, it's very reasonable to ask if so-called "price gouging" even exists at all.

• • • • •

Let's assume (this is a stretch) that no politicians have any desire to control prices just for the sake of (a) empowering themselves, or (b) making themselves look like they care *deeply* about voters, so they'll be reelected. Let's also assume that we all want the poor to be taken care of and for economies to run in the best way possible for everybody. The question becomes this, then:

Which method works better?

Is it (a) to leave people alone to determine their own prices as they buy and sell goods and services—and *compete*, so prices drop for consumers, which helps the poor, or (b) to put the government in charge of it?

> So-called "price gouging" ensures that products in high demand are available to those who need them the most.

Business owners work constantly to make sure that their prices are as "correct" as possible and result in the most sales, without losing money. And buyers can spend hours trying to find the best price, deciding sometimes whether they will pay more for a product because they're happy with a certain feature or convenience or other aspect, even though that particular product might not be the lowest-priced item available.

Big-government advocates often claim that sellers have all the power when it comes to pricing: "They can charge whatever they want, and the consumer has to pay!" But that's absolute nonsense.

Buyers wield an immense amount of power over what prices items sell for. If they don't think a good or service is worth the price, they buy less of it, they buy an alternative, or they don't buy it at all. And it does no good at all for sellers to have a load of overpriced items sitting around on their shelves, not being sold.

What Do You Think?

1. How is determining prices outside the ability of government planners?
2. Define *price controls*. What do governments *claim* they're trying to do with them? What happens instead?
3. For what other reasons are price controls immoral?
4. Explain how (a) defining "price gouging" is arrogant, (b) "price gouging" doesn't really exist, and (c) "price gouging" makes products in high demand available to those who need them most.

7.3 – Grocery Stores and the DMV

A person can walk into a grocery store any day of the week and think, *Wow, look at all the food and household items for sale here! Everything is so colorful and clean and neatly arranged up and down the aisles. How on earth do they* **do** *it?* That same person can also walk into any Department of Motor Vehicles office in America and think, *Wow, the workers here are so friendly and efficient! And the atmosphere is so welcoming and pleasant! How on earth do they* **do** *it?*

Question: What can we deduce from the above reactions?

Answer: We can deduce that that person has recently been hit on the head with a shovel. How? Because DMV agencies are notorious for their gloomy, slow, drab, inefficient environments.

• • • • •

 Today we'll read the article "Why Grocery Stores Run So Much More Efficiently Than DMVs," by author and economics professor Walter Block. Take notes on this article, and bring them to class next week! (You can access the article by taking a picture of that QR code with your smartphone, or searching the Internet for the article's title—including the author's name.)

7.4 – "I, Pencil" • Quiz 5

Leonard E. Read (1898-1983), the founder of the Foundation for Economic Education, wrote the following fun and instructive essay, "I, Pencil," in 1958.

• • • • •

I am a lead pencil—the ordinary wooden pencil familiar to all boys and girls and adults who can read and write. Writing is both my vocation and my avocation [job and calling]; that's all I do.

You may wonder why I should write a genealogy. Well, to begin with, my story is interesting. And, next, I am a mystery —more so than a tree or a sunset or even a flash of lightning. But, sadly, I am taken for granted by those who use me, as if I were a mere incident and without background. This supercilious [arrogant] attitude relegates me to the level of the commonplace. This is a species of the grievous error in which mankind cannot too long persist without peril. For, the wise G. K. Chesterton observed, "We are perishing for want of wonder, not for want of wonders."

I, Pencil, simple though I appear to be, merit your wonder and awe, a claim I shall attempt to prove. In fact, if you can understand me—no, that's too much to ask of anyone—if you can become aware of the miraculousness which I symbolize, you can help save the freedom mankind is so unhappily losing. I have a profound lesson to teach. And I can teach this lesson better than can an automobile or an airplane or a mechanical dishwasher because—well, because I am seemingly so simple.

Simple? Yet not a single person on the face of this earth knows how to make me. This sounds fantastic, doesn't it? Especially when it is realized that there are about one and one-half billion of my kind produced in the USA each year.

Pick me up and look me over. What do you see? Not much meets the eye—there's some wood, lacquer, the printed labeling, graphite lead, a bit of metal, and an eraser.

Innumerable Antecedents

Just as you cannot trace your family tree back very far, so is it impossible for me to name and explain all my antecedents [ancestors]. But I would like to suggest enough of them to impress upon you the richness and complexity of my background.

My family tree begins with what in fact is a tree, a cedar of straight grain that grows in Northern California and Oregon. Now contemplate all the saws and trucks and rope and the countless other gear used in harvesting and carting the cedar logs to the railroad siding. Think of all the persons and the numberless skills that went into their fabrication: the mining of ore, the making of steel and its refinement into saws, axes, motors; the growing of hemp and bringing it through all the stages to heavy and strong rope; the logging camps with their beds and mess halls, the cookery and the raising of all the foods. Why, untold thousands of persons had a hand in every cup of coffee the loggers drink!

The logs are shipped to a mill in San Leandro, California. Can you imagine the individuals who make flat cars and rails and railroad engines and who construct and install the communication systems incidental thereto? These legions are among my antecedents.

Consider the millwork in San Leandro. The cedar logs are cut into small, pencil-length slats less than one-fourth of an inch in thickness. These are kiln dried and then tinted for the same reason women put rouge on their faces. People prefer that I look pretty, not a pallid white. The slats are waxed and kiln dried again. How many skills went into the making of the tint and the kilns, into supplying the heat, the light and power, the belts, motors, and all the other things a mill requires? Sweepers in the mill among my ancestors? Yes, and included are the men who poured the concrete for the dam of a Pacific Gas & Electric Company hydroplant which supplies the mill's power!

Don't overlook the ancestors present and distant who have a hand in transporting sixty carloads of slats across the nation.

Once in the pencil factory—$4,000,000 [around $40 million today] in machinery and building, all capital accumulated by thrifty and saving parents of mine—each slat is given eight grooves by a complex machine, after which another machine lays leads in every other slat, applies glue, and places another slat atop—a lead sandwich, so to speak. Seven brothers and I are mechanically carved from this "wood-clinched" sandwich.

My "lead" itself—it contains no lead at all—is complex. The graphite is mined in Ceylon [Sri Lanka]. Consider these miners and those who make their many tools and the makers of the paper sacks in which the graphite is shipped and those who make the string that ties the sacks and those who put them aboard ships and those who make the ships. Even the lighthouse keepers along the way assisted in my birth—and the harbor pilots.

The graphite is mixed with clay from Mississippi in which ammonium hydroxide is used in...refining....Then wetting agents are added such as sulfonated tallow—animal fats chemically reacted with sulfuric acid. After passing through numerous machines, the mixture finally appears as endless extrusions—as from a sausage grinder—cut to size, dried, and baked for several hours at 1,850 degrees Fahrenheit. To increase their strength and smoothness the leads are then treated with a hot mixture which includes candelilla wax from Mexico, paraffin wax, and hydrogenated natural fats.

My cedar receives six coats of lacquer. Do you know all the ingredients of lacquer? Who would think that the growers of castor beans and the refiners of castor oil are a part of it? They are. Why, even the processes by which the lacquer is made a beautiful yellow involve the skills of more persons than one can enumerate!

Observe the labeling. That's a film formed by applying heat to carbon black mixed with resins. How do you make resins and what, pray, is carbon black?

My bit of metal—the ferrule—is brass. Think of all the persons who mine zinc and copper and those who have the skills to make shiny sheet brass from these products of nature. Those black rings on my ferrule are black nickel. What is black nickel and how is it applied? The complete story of why the center of my ferrule has no black nickel on it would take pages to explain.

Then there's my crowning glory, inelegantly referred to in the trade as "the plug," the part man uses to erase the errors he makes with me. An ingredient called "factice" is what does the erasing. It is a rubber-like product made by reacting rapeseed oil from the Dutch East Indies [Indonesia] with sulfur chloride. Rubber, contrary to the common notion, is only for binding purposes. Then, too, there are numerous vulcanizing and accelerating agents. The pumice comes from Italy; and the pigment which gives "the plug" its color is cadmium sulfide.

No One Knows

Does anyone wish to challenge my earlier assertion that no single person on the face of this earth knows how to make me?

Actually, millions of human beings have had a hand in my creation, no one of whom even knows more than a very few of the others. Now, you may say that I go too far in relating the picker of a coffee berry in far-off Brazil and food growers elsewhere to my creation; that this is an extreme position. I shall stand by my claim. There isn't a single person in all these millions, including the president of the pencil company, who contributes more than a tiny, infinitesimal bit of know-how. From the standpoint of know-how the only difference be-tween the miner of graphite in Ceylon and the logger in Oregon is in the type of know-how. Neither the miner nor the logger can be dispensed with, any more than can the chemist at the factory or the worker in the oil field—paraffin being a by-product of petroleum.

Here is an astounding fact: Neither the worker in the oil field nor the chemist nor the digger of graphite or clay nor any who mans or makes the ships or trains or trucks nor the one who runs the machine that does the knurling on my bit of metal nor the president of the company performs his singular task because he wants me. Each one wants me less, perhaps, than does a child in the first grade. Indeed, there are some among this vast multitude who never saw a pencil nor would they know how to use one. Their motivation is other than me. Perhaps it is something like this: Each of these millions sees that he can thus exchange his tiny know-how for the goods and services he needs or wants. I may or may not be among these items.

No Master Mind
There is a fact still more astounding: The absence of a master mind, of anyone dictating or forcibly directing these countless actions which bring me into being. No trace of such a person can be found. Instead, we find the Invisible Hand at work. This is the mystery to which I earlier referred.

It has been said that "only God can make a tree." Why do we agree with this? Isn't it because we realize that we ourselves could not make one? Indeed, can we even describe a tree? We cannot, except in superficial terms. We can say, for instance, that a certain molecular configuration manifests itself as a tree. But what mind is there among men that could even record, let alone direct, the constant changes in molecules that transpire in the life span of a tree? Such a feat is utterly unthinkable!

I, Pencil, am a complex combination of miracles: a tree, zinc, copper, graphite, and so on. But to these miracles which manifest themselves in nature an even more extraordinary miracle has been added: the configuration of creative human energies—millions of tiny know-hows configurating naturally and spontaneously in response to human necessity and desire and in the absence of any human masterminding! Since only God can make a tree, I insist that only God could make me. Man can no more direct these millions of know-hows to bring me into being than he can put molecules together to create a tree.

The above is what I meant when writing, "If you can become aware of the miraculousness which I symbolize, you can help save the freedom mankind is so unhappily losing." For, if one is aware that these know-hows will naturally, yes, automatically, arrange themselves into creative and productive patterns in response to human necessity and demand—that is, in the absence of governmental or any other coercive masterminding—then one will possess an absolutely essential ingredient for freedom: a faith in free people. Freedom is impossible without this faith.

Once government has had a monopoly of a creative activity such, for instance, as the delivery of the mails, most individuals will believe that the mails could not be efficiently delivered by men acting freely. And here is the reason: Each one acknowledges that he himself doesn't know how to do all the things incident to mail delivery. He also recognizes that no other individual could do it. These assumptions are correct. No individual possesses enough know-how to perform a nation's mail delivery any more than any individual possesses enough know-how to make a pencil. Now, in the absence of faith in free people—in the unawareness that millions of tiny know-hows would naturally and miraculously form and cooperate to satisfy this necessity—the individual cannot help but reach the erroneous conclusion that mail can be delivered only by governmental "masterminding."

Testimony Galore

If I, Pencil, were the only item that could offer testimony on what men and women can accomplish when free to try, then those with little faith would have a fair case. However, there is testimony galore; it's all about us and on every hand. Mail delivery is exceedingly simple when compared, for instance, to the making of an automobile or a calculating machine or a grain combine or a milling machine or to tens of thousands of other things. Delivery? Why, in this area where men have been left free to try, they deliver the human voice around the world in less than one second; they deliver an event visually and in motion to any person's home when it is happening; they deliver 150 passengers from Seattle to Baltimore in less than four hours; they deliver gas from Texas to one's range or furnace in New York at unbelievably low rates and without subsidy [government funding via taxpayers]; they deliver each four pounds of oil from the Persian Gulf to our Eastern Seaboard—halfway around the world—for less money than the government charges for delivering a one-ounce letter across the street!

The lesson I have to teach is this: Leave all creative energies uninhibited. Merely organize society to act in harmony with this lesson. Let society's legal apparatus remove all obstacles the best it can. Permit these creative know-hows freely to flow. Have faith that free men and women will respond to the Invisible Hand. This faith will be confirmed. I, Pencil, seemingly simple though I am, offer the miracle of my creation as testimony that this is a practical faith, as practical as the sun, the rain, a cedar tree, the good earth.

What Do You Think?

1. Explain this quote from "I, Pencil": "Neither the worker in the oil field nor the chemist nor the digger of graphite or clay nor any who mans or makes the ships or trains or trucks nor the one who runs the machine that does the knurling on my bit of metal nor the president of the company performs his singular task because he wants me."

2. Read says, "Once government has had a monopoly of a creative activity such, for instance, as the delivery of the mails, most individuals will believe that the mails could not be efficiently delivered by men acting freely. And here is the reason: Each one acknowledges that he himself doesn't know how to do all the things incident to mail delivery. He also recognizes that no other individual could do it." What would happen if the U. S. Post Office shut down?

3. Name a modern technology or product that's much more complicated than a pencil that is manufactured by complete strangers who don't know anything more than how to produce their part of the product.

4. Look up the term "Invisible Hand," which Read refers to several times in this essay. Where did the term come from, what does it mean, and what does it have to do with "I, Pencil"? →

Take Quiz 5 (online or in-person students only).
Feel free to use your notes, but there is a time limit!

8.1 – Government Spending and Waste

Other People's Money vs. <u>Your</u> Money

What many often refer to as "government spending" isn't really government spending at all. As we've seen, governments get money in three ways: taxing, borrowing, or inflating. These methods contrast to how most of us have to get *our* money: by waking up early in the morning, putting on our old work clothes and a pair of work gloves, rolling up our sleeves, and stealing it from Mom's purse while she's still asleep.

No, no, no; of course, there is no way on *earth* that we would for *any* reason *ever* do that in a million years, probably. The correct answer is, obviously, that most of us have to *work* for our money and save it. Not everybody has to work for it, of course. You might, for example, have some wealthy friends or relatives who barely notice or care when their parents buy them luxurious items like expensive athletic shoes, or a swimming pool, or a *good* economics book. But *your* parents, on the other hand, might buy your shoes at a garage sale, tell you to go swim in the creek, and get you a poor-quality economics book like...well, you know.[52]

The point: When you *work* for your money, it's more painful to part with it, and you're more scrupulous in how you spend it. That wad of cash you clutch in your hand after pulling weeds or babysitting children—and those figures on your bank statement—represent *work*. When you spend earned money on an item, sometimes you can even visualize how many hours it took you to earn that item as you hand the money across the counter to the seller. When I was

---

[52] Trust me on this: Years later, you will thank your parents for not giving you everything you want (except for the economics book part; that will cause severe, lifelong trauma).

11, for example, I wanted a new bike. To earn the money for it, for several months I mowed, raked, and bagged grass in the Florida summer heat (average temperature: approximately 257 degrees). That red ten-speed, which cost me $69.88 (I'll never forget that number), meant a lot to me—more than some of my friends' bikes did to them, since their parents bought those bikes for them. In the same way, since government-money spenders don't *earn* the money they spend, they're more careless with it, and they waste much of it. Examples of this waste litter our nation:

- **The Post Office** – The U. S. Post Office, mentioned in "I, Pencil" last week, is famous for its slowness, long lines, inconvenient opening hours, poor customer service, lost or stolen packages, and general inferiority to other shipping companies. And although the amount of tax-payer money pumped into the USPS increases every year, it loses *billions* of dollars every year, including $7.6 billion in 2020 and $6.9 billion in 2021![53]

- **The Education System** – The bloated, expensive U. S. education system has recently lost millions of students to homeschooling and private schools, as increasing numbers of parents refuse to send their children to be muzzled with masks, force-fed racist/socialist/anti-Christian teachings, and relentlessly taught to question their gender. And since fewer students are attending government schools, spending on those schools has decreased, right?

    Wrong! U. S. educational institutions continue to increase spending.[54] In fact, in 2021 government spent an average of $15,120 per student per year. *This is four times as much as it was in 1960, even adjusted for inflation.*[55, 56] Do you think today's students are four times more educated than they were in 1960? Neither do I; in fact, you could argue they're four times *less* educated. What could a homeschooling family do with $15,000 per student per year? Much more than a government school, that's for sure.

- **Coronavirus "Stimulus" Spending** – The $6 trillion in so-called "rescue funds" that the U. S. government doled out in 2021 (that's *trillion*, not *billion*), supposedly to assist with the COVID-19 "crisis," was packed with fraud and waste. Among those who received checks from the government were 19,000 Americans who made at least $1 million the previous year, with thousands of those making $5 million, $10 million, and even more. Other recipients of these funds did all kinds of dishonest things with the money: buying pricy sports cars, getting million-dollar loans, and inventing compa-

---

[53] "U. S. Postal Service Reports Fiscal Year 2021 Results," U. S. P. S., November 20, 2021, https://about.usps.com/newsroom/national-releases/2021/1110-usps-reports-fiscal-year-2021-results.htm.

[54] Jessica Marie Baumgartner, "Public Schools Are Spending Money Like Crazy, Despite Sharp Enrollment Declines," Intellectual Takeout, September 13, 2022, https://intellectualtakeout.org/2022/09/public-schools-are-spending-money-like-crazy-despite-sharp-enrollment-declines.

[55] Melanie Hanson, "U. S. Public Education Spending Statistics," *Education Data Initiative*, June 15, 2022, https://educationdata.org/public-education-spending-statistics.

[56] Corey A. DeAngelis, "Inflation-Adjusted K-12 Education Spending Per Student Has Increased by 280 Percent Since 1960," *Reason*, June 15, 2020, https://reason.org/commentary/inflation-adjusted-k-12-education-spending-per-student-has-increased-by-280-percent-since-1960.

nies that—if you want to get *picky* about it—didn't actually exist.[57, 58] *And that's just the fraud we **know** about.* There's no telling how much else of the money ended up being wasted or stolen.

You Want <u>How</u> Much for That Stapler?

I'm not exactly—nor ever *have* been—the savviest shopper in the world; my wife Julie leaves me in the dust in that department. Over the last many years, however, since I started teaching homeschool classes to teenagers full time, I have had to buy many items helpful to my business (paper, pens, staplers, aspirin, tasers, etc.). One head-scratching fact became apparent to me as I compared prices of office supplies at various office supply stores...to the same items found at department stores. And that fact was this: These office supply items were often *more expensive* at the office supply stores! I couldn't figure out for a long time *why* this was the case. My thoughts went like this:

> Aren't office supply stores supposed to **specialize** in...office supplies? Aren't they ordering way more of these types of supplies than other stores? If they're ordering **more** of these supplies, they should be getting them at better prices, so why can't they sell them more cheaply than other stores who **don't** specialize in office supplies?

Then one day the answer hit me. I remembered that before I started teaching, I worked for several companies that allowed employees to order office supplies for themselves. Our managers told us that we could pick out items from one of those three-inch thick office supply catalogues (you probably know the type I'm talking about—one of those glossy, full-color catalogues heavy enough that if thrown accurately, could bring down a full-grown moose). And what the managers meant, of course, when they told us we could pick out items from the catalogue was that *the company would pay for anything we ordered from it*. Now, here's a quick question for you:

Do you think that we employees were *more* careful or *less* careful about the money we spent for supplies than if we had to spend our *own* money?

You guessed it! (I hope.) And that's the same basic reason that government wastes billions of dollars every year: **Government officials aren't spending their *own* money, so they're nowhere near as careful in how they spend it.**

---

[57] Brian Faler, "Unemployment Assistance to Millionaires Soared During Pandemic," November 22, 2022, politico.com/news/2022/11/22/unemployment-assistance-millionaires-covid-pandemic-2020-00070446.
[58] Tony Room, "'Immense Fraud' Creates Immense Task for Washington As It Tries to Tighten Scrutiny of $6 Trillion in Emergency Coronavirus Spending," *Washington Post*, February 17, 2022, washingtonpost.com/us-policy/2022/02/17/stimulus-aid-oversight-fraud.

Being more careful of how we spend our *own* money is just human nature. It's related to how humans look out for their own interests first, and on a large scale it's nearly as certain as the law of gravity.

"Here's a free bike!" "Here's a free swimming pool!" "Here's a free economics book!" Government officials spending taxpayer money is the same concept as those offers, just billions of times worse. Consider this: If somebody told you that you could regularly buy items, and somebody *else* would pay for those items, how careful would *you* be about spending that money?

Not too pretty to think about, is it?

"Clean" Energy, Candy, and Cigarettes

Remember how Austrian and Keynesian economists differ? Austrians believe that economies grow best with no government interference—except for threatening or punishing fraud or violence; Keynesians believe that government spending "stimulates" the economy. (Keynesians thought, for example, that the "Coronavirus Rescue Spending" plan was a brilliant idea.)o But they blunder greatly when they look at government spending. Why? *Because they focus on only what is **seen**,* as Frederic Bastiat pointed out—like a person who sees a window get smashed and claims it's "good for the economy," since he looks only at the glass maker, who benefits from it.

Here's another example of that mindset. In 2012, an editorial column in *The New York Times* said this, in part:

> The federal government has given generously to the clean energy industry over the last few years, funneling billions of dollars in grants, loans, and tax breaks to renewable power sources like wind and solar, biofuels, and electric vehicles. "Clean tech" has been good in return. During the recession, it was one of the few sectors to add jobs.[59]

But as Queen Elizabeth famously said to George Washington after they defeated the Nazis during the War of 1812: "Well, DUH!"

Of COURSE "clean tech" jobs increased, even during that recession! The government *gave* that industry billions of dollars *taken from other taxpayers*; what in the world did that *Times* writer *think* was going to happen? Reading that statement is like hearing this conversation:

> **Roy:** My convenience store business has been *booming*! That seventh-grade kid Rodney Stickle has been buying *tons* of candy and cigarettes for himself and his friends.
>
> **Ann:** Wait a minute...you said it was Rodney *Stickle*? The *bully*? He's been stealing lunch money from kids in all the local neighborhoods for weeks!
>
> **Roy:** Get out of my store.

---

[59] "The End of Clean Energy Subsidies?", Editorial, *The New York Times*, May 5, 2012, nytimes.com/2012/05/06/opinion/sunday/the-end-of-clean-energy-subsidies.html.

In other words, it's ridiculous for the *New York Times* to gush about how wonderful it is for that the "clean energy" industry grew during a recession, since *the very reason it grew is because the government plundered funds from many other industries to pay for it!* It's a classic example of Bastiat's "That Which Is Seen" vs. "That Which Is Not Seen" scenario. One thing's for sure: the *Times* will never publish articles with *these* headlines, which could easily be related to that "clean energy" story:

ONE MILLION FEWER PAIRS OF SHOES MANUFACTURED, DUE TO HIGHER TAXES FOR "CLEAN ENERGY"

GOVERNMENT SPENDING ON ELECTRIC VEHICLES LEAVES 50,000 BUSINESSES UNABLE TO HIRE NEW EMPLOYEES

AFTER TAX INCREASES, FEWER DOLLARS TO INVEST MEANS NO NEW MACHINERY FOR NOW-POORER BEET FARMERS

Similarly, with the example of the coronavirus spending bill previously mentioned, its supporters say, "Look! Americans are getting checks in the mail, and they'll be able to spend them to buy things; it will help the economy!" But here's a question that ought to be asked:

Where is all this money really coming from?

If it's *taxation*, then Americans will have trillions of dollars less to spend on *other* items that they want to buy and invest in, since that money will have been plundered from them. (And nobody will actually *see* fewer customers buying goods or services like shoes or food or computers.) And if it *is* being taxed... what, exactly, is the point? How does it make any sense to take money from Americans, then turn around and give the money right back to them?

If the money is coming from *inflation*, then the value of Americans' money will shrink in the future—and the ones who get the "new money" first and spend it will make out like bandits *at the expense of others*, remember.

And if the "government" money handouts are *borrowed*, that money will one day have to be repaid—with interest.

Every dollar spent by the government is (a) taken away from taxpayers, and (b) spent more wastefully. Imagine, for example what would happen if the $15,000 that government schools spend on average per student every year were *not* taxed away. Would parents with "school-aged" children spend, on average, $15,000 for each one, just more efficiently?

Are you kidding? They'd spend *way* less, *and* the private schools or tutors they spent it on would also leave government schools in their dust. Every dollar left over from the $15,000 per student would be spent more wisely or invested. Unlike *government* spenders, businesses want to be as efficient as possible, to lower costs and maximize profits. *Bureaucrats have no such incentive.*

And who are "bureaucrats"? We'll talk more about them tomorrow.

What Do You Think?

1. Why is government spending inherently more wasteful?
2. Explain the basic economic mistake made by someone who says, "Look at the jobs created by this government program! How can you be against it?" How does this relate to the neighborhood bully example?
3. What kind of twisted incentive do you think it would offer a government agency if, for example, someone reviewed that agency and said, "We gave your department a $5 million budget last year, but you only spent $4 million, so we'll just have to knock that down to $4 million for next year's budget"?
4. In October 2022, San Francisco's city government approved the building of a public toilet in a town square. The toilet—*which was only 150 square feet*—cost *$1.7 million*, and wasn't scheduled to be installed *for more than two years*, in 2025.[60] Two questions: (a) How does this incident illustrate the main idea of this section, and (b) what other questions about the suspicious nature of this agreement can you think of?

8.2 – The Curse of Bureaucrats

What Makes a Bureaucrat?

You've surely heard of and are familiar with the government term *democracy* (rule with input from the people or rule by a majority of the people), and *aristocracy* (rule by an elite class, or by the few). That brings us to the term **bureaucracy**.

The term *bureau* means "office," like the Federal *Bureau* of Investigation, or FBI. A bureaucracy is rule by a system of government offices, and those employed by bureaucracies are often referred to as *bureaucrats*.[61]

Bureaucrats—that is, government employees in general—have a well-deserved reputation (although, of course, exceptions exist) for being meddlesome, conceited, inflexible, lazy, and maybe even worse, *not* lazy. And what's worse about a bureaucrat who *isn't* lazy?

Well, to those forced to deal with irritating government departments, if a bureaucrat at some agency like the Department of Ice Cream Quality Assurance

---

[60] Heather Knight, "S. F. Is Spending $1.7 Million on One Public Toilet: 'What Are They Making It Out Of: Gold?'", October 19, 2022, *San Francisco Chronicle*, sfchronicle.com/sf/bayarea/heatherknight/article/million-dollar-toilet-17518443.php.

[61] Those who have had experience with bureaucrats often pronounce that word in the same tone of voice you would use to say "KID-ney stone."

did nothing but sit at his desk and play computer games all day, it would certainly be a waste of taxpayer money. But at least that bureaucrat wouldn't be actively looking for ways to *interfere* in ice cream sellers' businesses and make their jobs unnecessarily harder or costlier. But an active, arrogant bureaucrat at that department might think that he knew more about the ice cream industry than the ice cream makers and sellers themselves, and then imagine that he had a right to meddle in it:

> *Maybe I should push for new laws about how cold ice cream trucks have to be....Or maybe I should come up with a new list of requirements that all ice cream makers have to check off every month....Or maybe I should make ice cream makers go through training classes every year....Or maybe I should try to force ice cream makers to provide dairy-free choices to all customers....Or maybe I should...*

You get the picture. We've already reviewed how in general grocery stores are run much more efficiently than DMV offices. And yesterday we looked at the comparative lack of concern bureaucrats—and practically all humans, for that matter—show about how they spend money that isn't theirs. For another take on why bureaucrats are so infuriating, look at Ludwig von Mises's take on them. In his 1944 book *Bureaucracy*, Mises observes this:

> Bureaucratic management is management bound to comply with detailed rules and regulations fixed by the authority of a superior body. The task of the bureaucrat is to perform what these rules and regulations order him to do. His discretion to act according to his own best conviction is seriously restricted by them.[62]

In other words, bureaucrats are known for their thoughtless rule-following—even if these rules are harmful, wasteful, pointless, or just plain stupid. Sometimes when we deal with bureaucrats and their incompetence and apathy, it's just an annoying inconvenience, a waste of time, and/or a waste of money. Other times, however, bureaucracies are deadly. When 100 government police officers, for example, can't stop in less than an hour a murderer who kills several innocent mall shoppers, and a single 22-year-old with a gun can,[63] that's serious and tragic.

Three Characteristics of Bureaucracies and Bureaucrats

Here are three common characteristics about government bureaucracies, and the bureaucrats they employ:

1. **Enormously High Numbers** – In the United States in 2021, state and local governments combined to employ 18.83 million persons, and the United States government employed 2.85 mil-

---

[62] Ludwig von Mises, *Bureaucracy* (Yale University Press, 1944), 45.
[63] "Gunman Kills 3 in Indiana Mall Before Being Fatally Shot by an Armed Bystander: What We Know," *USA Today*, July 18, 2022, usatoday.com/story/news/nation/2022/07/18/ greenwood-park-mall-shooting-indianapolis-indiana/10084818002.

lion persons (21.7 million total).[64] In the same year, there were 127.2 million *total* full-time employees in America.[65] Look at that total again. Do you realize what that means? It means that *approximately 17 percent of all employees in the United States are employed by the government*! Now, visualize living in a little neighborhood with six families (or houses). Next, visualize that on average, *five of those families in your neighborhood work full time to pay the salary of that sixth neighbor.* Finally, visualize calm, soothing waves lapping up on the shore, so you won't be tempted to punch that sixth neighbor in the nose.

2. **Crippling Costs** – A 2021 study showed that the cost of bureaucracy and regulation in the U. S.—not including taxes—was approximately $1.9 trillion. This refers to all the time wasted and expenses that businesses incur just to comply with tens of thousands of government laws and policies. This $1.9 trillion translates to a cost of over $14,000 per family that year—again, *not* in taxes, but in government regulations.[66] Examples of ridiculous and troublesome regulations include requiring every computer repair technician to have a private investigator's license (Texas), forcing all bloggers to buy a $300 "business privilege license" to operate (Philadelphia), requiring daycare centers to brush every child's teeth after lunch (Massachusetts), and forcing companies who go out of business to *buy a license before they are allowed to* (Milwaukee).[67] These regulations would be almost funny if business owners didn't have to waste so much time and money complying with them.

3. **Inflated Salaries** – The average salary of an American bureaucrat, whether working for the U. S. government or for a state government, has long been much higher than the average salary of an American worker (this holds true in other nations, too). Even back in 2010, for example, government bureaucrats in America took home on average approximately $123,000 in pay and benefits, which is *twice* what the average American worker made per year, which was around $61,000.[68] Now, some might ask this:

---

[64] Erin Duffin, "Number of Governmental Employees in the U. S. from 1982 to 2021," *Statista*, June 21, 2022, statista.com/statistics/204535/number-of-governmental- employees-in-the-us.
[65] "Number of Full-time Employees in the United States from 1990 to 2021," *Statista*, July 27, 2022, statista.com/statistics/192356/number-of-full-time-employees-in-the-usa-since-1990.
[66] Clyde Wayne Crews, "Ten Thousand Commandments 2021," Competitive Enterprise Institute, June 30, 2021, https://cei.org/studies/ten-thousand-commandments-2021.
[67] Michael Snyder, "12 Ridiculous Government Regulations That Are Almost Too Bizarre to Believe," *Business Insider*, November 12, 2010, businessinsider.com/ridiculous-regulations-big-government-2010-11.
[68] John Tamny, "Government Pay: Now for the Really Bad News," *Forbes*, August 30, 2010, forbes.com/2010/08/27/government-jobs-wages-innovation-opinions-columnists-john-tamny.html. (Government employees also typically receive many more paid holidays than the av-

"But what about *teachers*?" Well, teacher pay compares quite favorably. The average teacher's salary in the U. S. is roughly equal to the salary of a police officer, a plumber, a chemical plant system operator, or a real estate appraiser—and the average hourly pay rate of teachers rises considerably when the number of weeks worked per year is factored in.[69]

The power that bureaucrats wield to meddle in the lives of others, as well as their excessively high salaries, means that anybody who tries to shrink the bureaucracy is in for a battle. Bureaucrats will fight almost to the death to keep their positions, where they enjoy (a) high pay and (b) power over others. American economist Milton Friedman (1912-2006) once famously said, "There is nothing so permanent than a temporary government program."[70] Congressman Ron Paul also expressed a similar sentiment:

> Once government does become involved in something...inertia [inaction] tends to keep it there for good. People lose their political imagination. It becomes impossible to conceive of dealing with the matter in any other way. Repealing the new bureaucracy becomes unthinkable. Mythology about how terrible things were in the old days becomes the conventional wisdom. Meanwhile, the bureaucracy itself, with a vested interest in maintaining itself and increasing its funding, employs all the resources it can to ensuring that it gets a bigger budget next year, regardless of its performance. In fact, the worse it does, the more funding it is likely to get—exactly the opposite of what happens in the private sector, in which those who successfully meet the needs of their fellow men are rewarded with profits, and those who poorly anticipate consumer demand are punished with losses.[71]

What Do You Think?

1. Define the term *bureaucrat*.
2. List some characteristics of bureaucracies and bureaucrats.
3. How much did bureaucratic regulations on businesses cost the average American family in 2021?
4. What is the main difference between bureaucracies and private businesses, according to the passage from Ron Paul?

---

erage American worker, as well as a much more generous retirement plan, as well as other benefits and compensations.)
[69] Jeffrey Dorfman, "Low Teacher Pay and High Teacher Pay Are Both Myths," *Forbes*, August 7, 2014, forbes.com/sites/jeffreydorfman/2014/08/07/low-teacher-pay-and-high-teacher-pay-are-both-myths.
[70] Dr. Eamonn Butler, "Nothing Is So Permanent as a Temporary Government Program," August 13, 2010, Adam Smith Institute, adamsmith.org/blog/tax-spending/nothing-is-so-permanent-as-a-temporary-government-program.
[71] Ron Paul, *The Revolution* (Grand Central Publishing, 2008), 74.

8.3 – Public Works, Shovels, and Spoons

The following brilliant little essay, "Public Works," is taken from Frederic Bastiat's essay "That Which Is Seen, and That Which Is Not Seen." The term **public works** describes when a government tries to solve the issue of unemployment—but not by getting itself out of the way of those trying to make a living, which would be the most reasonable, sensible, effective thing to do. No, "public works" are government attempts to employ *one* group of workers by taxing *other* groups of workers and using that transferred money to "create jobs" for the unemployed. In about 800 words, Bastiat carves into mincemeat the notion that public works programs help the economy.

•••••

Public Works

Nothing is more natural than that a nation, after having assured itself that a project will benefit the community, should have it executed by means of a general tax. But I lose patience, I confess, when I hear this economic blunder advanced in support of such a project: "Besides, it will be a means of creating labor for the workmen."

The State opens a road, builds a palace, straightens a street, cuts a canal, and so gives work to certain workmen—*this is what is seen*. But it deprives certain other workmen of work—this is what *is not seen*.

The road is begun. A thousand workmen come every morning, leave every evening, and take their wages—this is certain. If the road had not been decreed, if the supplies had not been voted, these good people would have had neither work nor salary there; this also is certain.

But is this all? Does not the operation contain something else? At the moment when the law is adopted, do the millions descend miraculously on a moonbeam into the state treasury? In order that the transformation may be complete, as it is said, must not the State organize the *collection* of the money as well as the spending of it? Must it not set its tax-gatherers and taxpayers to work, the former to gather and the latter to pay?

Study the question, now, in both its elements. While you state the destination given by the State to the millions voted,

Where Money Comes From

do not neglect to state also the destination which the taxpayer would have given, but cannot now give, to the same. Then you will understand that a public enterprise is a coin with two sides. Upon one is engraved a laborer at work, with this device, *that which is seen*; on the other is a laborer out of work, with the device, *that which is not seen*.

The false claim which this work is intended to refute is the more dangerous when applied to public works, inasmuch as it serves to justify the most reckless enterprises and extravagance. When a railroad or a bridge is of real use, it is sufficient to mention this usefulness. But if it does not exist, what do they say? They resort to this absurdity: "We must find work for the workmen."

Accordingly, orders are given that the drains in the Champ-de-Mars[72] be made and unmade. The great Napoleon, it is said, thought he was doing a very charitable work by causing ditches to be made and then filled up. He said, therefore, "What signifies the result? All we want is to see wealth spread among the laboring classes."

But let us go to the root of the matter. We are deceived by money. To demand the cooperation of all the citizens in a common work, in the form of money, is in reality to demand an agreement in kind; for everyone acquires, by his own labor, the sum to which he is taxed. Now, if all the citizens were to be called together, and made to execute, in conjunction, a work useful to all, this would be easily understood; their reward would be found in the results of the work itself.

But after having called them together, if you force them to make roads which no one will pass through, palaces which no one will inhabit, and this under the pretense of finding them work, it would be absurd, and they would have a right to argue, "With this labor we have nothing to do; we prefer working on our own ac-count."

A proceeding which consists in making the citizens cooperate in giving money, but not labor, does not, in any way, alter the general results. The only thing is, that the loss would react upon all parties. By the former, those whom the State employs, escape their part of the loss, by adding it to that which their fellowcitizens have already suffered.

There is an article in our constitution which says, "Society favors and enourages the development of labor—by the establishment of public works, by the

---

[72] a public park in Paris

State, the departments, and the parishes, as a means of employing persons who are in want of work."

As a temporary measure, on any emergency, during a hard winter, this interference with the taxpayers might have its use. It acts in the same way as securities. It adds nothing either to labor or to wages, but it takes labor and wages from ordinary times to give them, at a loss it is true, to times of difficulty.

As a permanent, general, systematic measure, it is nothing else than a ruinous mystification [confusion], an impossibility, which shows a little excited labor *which is seen*, and hides a great deal of prevented labor *which is not seen*.

· · · · ·

An incident related to Bastiat's above essay, which involves economist Milton Friedman, goes like this:

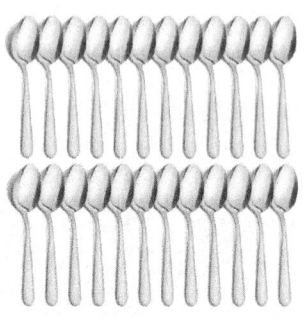

> While traveling by car during one of his many overseas travels, Professor Milton Friedman spotted scores of road builders moving earth with shovels instead of modern machinery. When he asked why powerful equipment wasn't used instead of so many laborers, his host told him it was to keep employment high in the construction industry. If they used tractors or modern road building equipment, fewer people would have jobs....[That] was his host's logic.
>
> "Then instead of shovels, why don't you give them spoons and create even more jobs?" Friedman inquired.[73]

What Do You Think?

1. Bastiat starts "Public Works" by saying a state project that employs some "deprives certain other workmen of work." <u>How</u> does a state project deprive others of work?
2. What in this essay is seen, and what is <u>not</u> seen?
3. How does the Milton Friedman "shovels and spoons" story fit in with Bastiat's "Public Works" essay?
4. Fill in the blanks: "The ___ of the ___ is the ___: a good ___ have all they that ___" (Psalm 111:10).

8.4 – CLAIM: "Monopolies Must Be <u>Stopped</u>!" • Quiz 6

From memory, mentally fill in the blanks of these verses about the purpose of government (you should be getting pretty good at these):

---

[73] Mark J. Perry, "Milton Friedman Shovels vs. Spoons Story," American Enterprise Institute, December 6, 2006, aei.org/carpe-diem/milton-friedman-shovels-vs-spoons-story.

- To *"remove ___ and ___, and execute ___ and ___"* (Ezekiel 45:9)
- To *"deliver the ___ out of the hand of the ___"* (Jeremiah 22:3)
- To punish *"___"* (1 Peter 2:13-14)
- To be a *"terror"* and *"revenger"* to *"___"* (Romans 13:4)

• • • • •

The Scenario: Imagine you live in a totally free market economy.[74] Next, imagine that you're sitting in a college economics class, and a student sitting next to you makes this claim:

> That WoodCo company has a *monopoly* on lumber in the western region of the U. S. The government needs to break up that monopoly; it's way too much power for a single company to have.

Answer the following questions—and if you're in my in-person or online class, be sure to bring your answers to our next class:

1. What exactly *is* a "monopoly"? (Quickly look up a definition.) At what *exact* percentage point of "owning" a market does a company become a "monopoly"? Does any person or committee really *know* that percentage? If not, what do you think about the likelihood that a government agency will be able to precisely define it?

2. How can a monopoly exist in a totally free economy? Who determines what market share a company has?

3. Can you think of any monopolies or near-monopolies *created by government*? In other words, what are some institutions you have little or no choice about having to use? How efficient are those government-created monopolies?

Take Quiz 6 (online or in-person students only). Feel free to use your notes, but there is a time limit!

9.1 – Test 3

If you're in my in-person or online Economics class, take Test 3 today. This test focuses on material from Weeks 6-8, but also might contain material from previous weeks. First review your notes, then take Test 3!

---

[74] Then, while you're at it, you might as well imagine a herd of purple unicorns flying around, and gluten-free brownies that taste as good as *real* brownies.

9.2 – Unintended Consequences: Potatoes and Cobras

Unintended Consequences: Definition and Examples

The Biblical model for government is to restrict it to threatening and executing judgement and justice upon evildoers: those who threaten, harm, or violate the lives, persons, property, and liberties of others. (It's possible I might have mentioned that before.)

This is also an instinctively sensible, reasonable position.

After all, we all certainly realize that *we* shouldn't steal from other individuals or violate their liberties or property rights. Likewise, we also ought to recognize that *governments* shouldn't do it either.

Government officials muddy this clear-cut issue, however, when they perform deeds that *appear* to be attempts to help others. We innately sense that the government ought to be "doing good" in some way, and sometimes it's easy to mistake government policies that fall *outside* the Biblical standard as legitimate, simply because they *appear* to be benevolent.

Which, of course, brings us to potatoes and cobras.

But not yet.

First, remember that we've seen several examples of what free-market economists call **unintended consequences**—unexpected results that occur when government planners implement economic policies:

- In Bastiat's "Public Works" example, the government employs (at taxpayer expense) a certain group of persons, but as a result of higher taxes to pay for this, *other* sellers make fewer sales and hire fewer employees, since taxpayers now have less to spend.

- Government officials who want to appear as if they're "doing something" pass anti-"price gouging" laws on products in high demand during an emergency like a hurricane or power outage. But this only hurts those buyers who really *need* those products, since (a) sellers are discouraged from producing more of those items, and (b) buyers snatch up more than they normally would.

- The government offers checks to "rescue" taxpayers from the effects of *other* ill-advised COVID-19 government policies, only to have many billions of dollars stolen and fraudulently snapped up.

Of course, we've also looked at one gigantic *positive* example of unintended consequences—but not by *government* action; do you remember what that example was? (Hint: It has to do with Adam Smith.)

Did you remember? Of course, it's the "invisible hand"—the concept that in a free market, when producers try to make as much money as possible for *themselves*, they inadvertently also enrich the lives of *others* by making goods and services more available, and cheaper.

Let's Play "Unintended Consequences"!

Next, let's try three rounds of Unintended Consequences, in which you try to deduce what unintended consequences result from a government action or policy. First, try two practice examples (the answers are at the bottom of the page):

Unintended Consequence A: Seat Belt Laws – Many state governments over several decades have passed "mandatory seat belt laws," with the goal of cutting down on car crash fatalities. (Sometimes these state governments post road signs that say things like "Click it or ticket.") Do you think these laws reduced car crash deaths? Why or why not? (Hint: How did many non-seat-belt-wearing drivers *drive* differently than they did before, after governments forced them to wear seat belts? Think about it before looking at the answer below.[75])

Unintended Consequence B: Obamacare Results – In 2010 Congress passed the "Affordable Care Act" (ACA), also known as "Obamacare." The ACA decreed that companies must pay for their employees' health insurance if those companies have 50 or more employees who work an average of 30 or more hours a week. What do you think happened to many employees' jobs in those companies, as well as the number of hours they worked per week? Think about it first before looking at the answer below![76]

---

[75] The laws did not reduce automobile fatalities, because drivers on the whole drove more recklessly, believing they were safer because they wore seat belts. (Ted Balaker, "Unbuckling Seat Belt Laws," Reason Foundation, May 27, 2004, https://reason.org/commentary/unbuckling-seat-belt-laws.)

[76] Many companies fired dozens, hundreds, or even thousands of employees, because they couldn't afford the additional cost, and many companies restricted formerly 40-hour-per-week em-

Three More Unintended Consequence Examples

Now try these! Read the following three cases, then see if you can deduce what unintended consequences resulted from the following government policies. (Treat these as your "What Do You Think?" review questions for today.)

To check your answers to the following cases, look up the article or video link attached to each example. (If you're in my in-person or online class, you don't have look up answers; we'll talk about the cases in class.)

Unintended Consequence Example #1: The 1973 Endangered Species Act. This law, passed in 1973, has prevented many American landowners from building on, cutting down trees on, clearing, or otherwise improving their property if a so-called "endangered species" was found to be living on or around it. The act was supposedly designed to protect those species. What do you think often happened to "endangered species" animals that landowners discovered on their property, when those landowners realized that they faced the permanent loss of the use of that land if those animals were found by bureaucrats?[77]

Unintended Consequence Example #2: Potatoes and the COVID-19 Hysteria. U. S. and state governments all over America hassled, threatened, heavily regulated, and/or shut down thousands of restaurants during the 2020-21 COVID-19 panic, supposedly to "save millions of lives" from a common virus that government officials later grudgingly admitted was a little *less* deadly than the yearly flu. Restaurants of all kinds, from five-star gourmet to fast food chains, serve potatoes that are cooked in many varieties. What do you think happened to many American farmers who grew potatoes for a living by selling their potatoes to those restaurants all over the country?[78]

Unintended Consequence Example #3: Killing Cobras. Our last unintended consequences example takes us to the city of Delhi, India, when it was under British rule in the nineteenth century. In Delhi, venomous cobras proliferated throughout the city's streets, and even invaded many homes. The governor of Delhi then "issued a bounty on cobra skins" to help rid the city of the nuisance. When residents realized that the government of Delhi would

---

ployees to working 29 hours a week so they wouldn't be forced to pay for those employees' insurance, obviously hurting the earnings of those employees. (Andrew Johnson, "100 Unintended Consequences of Obamacare," *Business Insider*, October 1, 2013, nationalreview.com/2013/10/100-unintended-consequences-obamacare-andrew-johnson.)

[77] Ronald Bailey, "Shoot, Shovel, and Shut Up," December 31, 2003, Reason, https://reason.com/2003/12/31/shoot-shovel-and-shut-up.

[78] "Why Millions of Pounds of Potatoes Are Being Thrown Away During the Pandemic," *Business Insider*, June 28, 2020, youtube.com/watch? v=ALtfQVbHtM0.

pay them for every cobra skin they brought to the governor, what do you think happened as a result?[79]

9.3 – Tariffs: Pickled Beets, Policies, and Plunder

Burgling Bargain Beet Buyers

Tariffs perfectly illustrate the kind of faulty and destructive economic thinking that Frederic Bastiat describes in "That Which Is Seen, and That Which Is Not Seen." But tariffs are not just irrational or flawed policies implemented by lawmakers "trying to do the right thing." Unfortunately, tariffs are also loaded with the potential for bribery and corruption involving companies and government officials.

What is a **tariff**? It's a tax on an imported product. For centuries, many government officials (and citizens as well) have erroneously believed that their prosperity depended greatly upon ensuring that the products *their* citizens produced were the ones purchased by their own nation's consumers—and other nations' consumers, instead of similar products made elsewhere. In other words, let's say that American government officials realize that U. S. consumers are buying French pickled beets, not American ones. "Horrors! We can't allow *that*!" those officials might say. "Why, that would create a terrible *imbalance of trade*, and harm our pickled beet industry, therefore damaging the American economy!"

Those U. S. officials then might enact a law that placed a tariff on pickled beets imported from France. Let's say that American pickled beets cost $2 per can, but French pickled beets cost $1 per can. A $2-per-can tariff is added to French pickled beets, making them $3 per can. Now most—if not all—American pickled beet buyers buy the American-produced pickled beets. "See?" claim the U. S. lawmakers. "We're protecting the American economy! Our pickled beet makers aren't losing their jobs to foreign companies. Also, the businesses *around* the pickled beet producers—grocery stores, shoe stores, gas stations, and so on—are benefiting, since the money those pickled beet producers earn will be spent at those stores."

But as you probably are aware, these officials have made a basic economic mistake. (We'll assume they're adding the tariff mistakenly, with purely unselfish intentions.) They're only looking at *one* group—or in this case, a few groups—, instead of *everyone* affected by these tariffs. Yes, the American pickled beet *producers* benefit, as are those merchants from whom they buy goods and services. But what about pickled beet *buyers*? Now they're forced

---

[79] "The Cobra Effect: Unintended Consequences in British India," WCBE 90.5 FM, WCBE Podcast Experience, October 4, 2021, wcbe.org/arts-life/2021-10-04/the-cobra-effect-unintended-consequences-in-british-india.

to pay more, and they lose out. Before the tariff was added to French pickled beets, a pickled beet buyer with two dollars had (a) a can of pickled beets, and (b) an extra dollar he could spend, save, or invest. After the tariff was added, that pickled beets buyer had (a) a can of pickled beets, and (b) nothing. Multiply that by millions of buyers, and the entire country is now poorer by millions of dollars—or even many billions, depending upon what items to which tariffs are added.

(And even if the tariff were $1 per can, which would make the price of American pickled beets the *same* as the French imports, pickled beet buyers would still lose out. Before, they had a chance to buy a can for $1. Now they must spend another dollar—a dollar they could have used elsewhere.)

Four Ways Tariffs Harm

Here are four reasons why tariffs are an overall harm to society:

1. **Tariffs make nations poorer overall, and they hurt the *poor* the worst.** As noted in above example, tariffs on products force consumers to pay more than they would have for products in a free market, in which those consumers would have bought from more efficient producers. And tariffs harm the poor more than others—first, because, as with inflation, the poor have less to spend to begin with, and second, because "the poor spend proportionally more on goods produced in other countries" than the rich do.[80] Tariffs are like taxes on the poor!

2. **Tariffs slow down economic progress.** Much of the reason why we in our modern economy enjoy technological advances like computers and cell phones is because *investors saved their money*, and they invested that money in high-tech ideas that produced the sophisticated machinery and gadgets that make life easier, safer, and even less painful. Tariffs rob millions of individuals of extra savings that investors would have otherwise had—but now are missing, since buyers must spend it on products they could have bought more cheaply otherwise. Those many *billions* of dollars per year are lost to less efficient producers, slowing down future investments in new technologies and inventions.

3. **Tariffs unjustifiably empower government.** It's possible I've mentioned this once (or even twice) already, but some government officials actually believe—without a shred of evidence—that they possess the magical ability to determine exactly *which* goods and services should be produced in an economy, how *much* of those items should be produced, and what *prices* should be charged for them. When a producer of pickled beets, for example, complains to lawmakers that he's losing money to foreign competition, this can be exciting to meddling bureaucrats who think, *Here's our chance to influence the economy the way we see fit!* But of course, those kinds of

---

[80] Johan Norberg, "Dead Wrong With Johan Norberg: Unequal Benefits of Trade," Free To Choose Network, youtube.com/watch?v=gF2zzX_1lOA.

legislators almost never come even close to acknowledging this *tiny* possibility: *You know, maybe we'd better wait on trying to meddle in the economy—we can't see other consequences this tariff might create.* No, these types of politicians simply prattle on about some kind of "imbalance of trade" created by those evil French pickled beet producers (the *villains*!), and how we "need to protect our local manufacturers." But here's what they're really saying:

A British Pro-Tariff Poster

> Too many of the people in "our country" are *wrongly* buying cheaper pickled beets from foreigners, since "our" pickled beet producers lack those foreign pickled beet producers' efficiency. Those buyers of the cheaper beets are *incorrect*, so we must *correct* them, since *we* know better than they do how they should spend their own money.[81]

For a politician—or even a group of them, regardless of how "smart" they are, or *think* they are—to claim to know when an "imbalance of trade" exists is absurd. If you asked 50 government planners, "At exactly what point does a nation have an 'imbalance of trade'?" you'd get 50 different answers. And let's say that by some miracle all 50 planners gave you the same answer. Next, you could ask this: "What is the *exact* list of products imported from other nations that we should place tariffs on, and the exact amounts and/or percentages of tariffs for each product?" If you get the same 50 answers to *that* question, I'll eat my hat, and my coat for dessert.

The point is that *nobody knows the answers to these questions*—just like we saw before that nobody knows the answer to this question: "When,

---

[81] It doesn't necessarily have to mean that foreign pickled beet producers are smarter or better workers. It might just be that beets simply grow better in other nations' climates. Or maybe beets grown in certain countries taste better, or increase your vocabulary, or give you softer, more manageable hair, or something.

exactly, are sellers just selling something for a high price, and when are they 'price gouging'?" There *are* individuals that generally know when prices are too high, and what items should be produced, and how many: *buyers and sellers in a free market.* They don't know all the answers perfectly, and they make mistakes, but they know infinitely better than any group of politicians that ever lived or will live.

And by the way, when enough pickled beet producers can join forces to pressure lawmakers to add a tariff to *their* product, what do *other* industries that are losing business to foreign producers try to do?

You guessed it!

And why shouldn't they? After all, if you believe that tariffs on *one* product are "helpful to the economy," why wouldn't tariffs on *all* foreign competition also be? Of course, even most politicians realize that would be ridiculous, but that pressure from outside groups can reinforce some bureaucrats' belief that *they*, as The Chosen Ones, possess the Mysterious Key of Knowledge that qualifies them to decide which imports should have tariffs added to them, so they can direct the economy to avoid that ghastly "imbalance of trade." But unfortunately, as these politicians are making those Big Decisions on which companies to favor, they become susceptible to one of the curses of government meddling in economies, which is the fact that...

4. **Tariffs—like many government economic policies—are often driven by bribery.** Government officials with even an modicum of self-awareness and humility realize that they don't know enough to determine which tariffs "ought to" be imposed on what products, so *they start acting politically and/or to benefit themselves.* (Remember man's nature!) That is, politicians in a steel-producing state will often push for steel tariffs, simply because those tariffs "protect jobs" in *that* state, which is made up of (Surprise!) many voters connected to the steel industry. A politician who votes *against* that tariff can face the wrath of unhappy voters who want their jobs protected from foreign competitors. Another common misdeed involving tariffs occurs like this:

> Company X lets Politician A know that if he arranges to have a tariff added to a bill that protects Company X's product from foreign competition, the company will reward him. Politician A arranges to have the tariff added to the bill: "It will save the jobs of our people!" he proclaims during a session of Congress. (Part of how Politician A arranges to have the tariff added to the bill is that he surreptitiously promises Politicians B, C, and D that he will vote to include items in that bill that benefit *their* states if they vote to include *his*.) When the bill becomes a law, Company X reaps millions, and after Politician A leaves Congress, Company X "hires" him at $3 million per year, as a "consultant." (Politicians B, C, and D also benefit, of course.)

Sweet for You, Sour for Us

To finish this section, let's look at the sugar industry in America, a glaring example of what's wrong with tariffs. **Americans pay about 41 percent more for sugar than the rest of the world.** Why? Because the U. S. government meddles in sugar production by—this is not a joke—*restricting the amount of sugar that Americans are allowed to buy from other nations*, unless a tariff is imposed. (At this point, once again, you might want to visualize calm, soothing waves lapping up on the shore, so you're not tempted to find one of these tariff-favoring politicians and punch him in the nose.) Also, the sugar industry—which produces only about two percent of all crops grown in America—spends 34 percent of all ~~bribery~~ "lobbying" dollars sent to lawmakers to influence the content of bills. Estimates on how much these plundering sugar restrictions and tariffs cost the U. S. economy range in the billions of dollars per year.[82] The Bible refers to that kind of activity by lobbyists and politicians this way:

> *A wicked man taketh a gift [bribe] out of the bosom to pervert the ways of judgment (Proverbs 17:23).*
>
> *The king by judgment establisheth the land: but he that receiveth gifts overthroweth it (Proverbs 29:4).*
>
> *Woe unto them that decree unrighteous decrees, and that write grievousness which they have prescribed (Isaiah 10:1).*

Once again, the Bible is correct—just like it's been for thousands of years!

What Do You Think?

1. Define *tariff*. How is a tariff an example of a flaw in economic reasoning?
2. How do tariffs introduce more corruption in government?
3. Explain in your own words the message of the tariff poster a few pages back. How could you answer the poster artist's belief?

9.4 – CLAIM: "You Support Greed and Selfishness!"

Fill in the blanks of the below verses from memory, which spell out the legitimate purposes of government:

- To *"remove ___ and ___, and execute ___ and ___"* (Ezekiel 45:9)
- To *"deliver the ___ out of the hand of the ___"* (Jeremiah 22:3)
- To punish *"___"* (1 Peter 2:13-14)

---

[82] Brian Riley, "The U. S. Sugar Program: Bad for Consumers, Bad for Agriculture, Bad for America," Americans for Tax Reform, April 18, 2012, heritage.org/agriculture/report/the-us-sugar-program-bad-consumers-bad-agriculture-and-bad-america.

- To be a *"terror"* and *"revenger"* to *"___"* (Romans 13:4)

• • • • •

The Scenario: During a class at your church, you have an opportunity to share a little of what you know about economics during the discussion. After class, one of your classmates who attends a government school says this to you:

> Aren't we supposed to act like *Christians*? I thought Christians believed that all mankind was *sinful*. How can you support an economic system like capitalism, which rewards *greed* and *selfishness*, and takes advantage of the poor? Isn't greed and selfishness supposed to be *sinful*?

Jot down a few ideas in your Economics notebook about how you could answer these questions, and if you're in my in-person or online class, bring them to our next class.

10.1 – Taxes and Exactions

The Proper Reason for Taxes

Government officials should limit their collection of taxes to pay for *necessary* government expenses like judges, police officers, courts, and other areas that help fulfill government's *proper* duties: to *"deliver the spoiled out of the hand of the oppressor,"* to punish *"evildoers,"* and to be a *"terror"* and a *"revenger"* to *"evil."* And to point this out once again, the proper, Biblical functions of government do *not* include commonly accepted matters such as roads, libraries, schools, charities, health care, housing, and so on.

And remember Ezekiel 45:9, which explains what God expects from rulers: *"Thus saith the Lord GOD; 'Let it suffice you, O princes of Israel: remove violence and spoil, and execute judgment and justice....'"* That verse's second part, which we haven't looked at yet, reads like this (bold added):

> *"...take away your **exactions** from my people,"* saith the Lord GOD.

An **exaction** is an unjust tax or a property theft by a government official. The word *exaction* is related to the verb **exact**, which is defined this way in Webster's 1828 *American Dictionary of the English Language*:

- To force or compel to pay or yield; to demand or require authoritatively; to extort by means of authority or without pity or justice. It is an offense for an officer to *exact* illegal or unreasonable fees. It is customary for conquerors to *exact* tribute or contributions from conquered countries.

- To demand....Princes *exact* obedience of their subjects. The laws of God *exact* obedience from all men....
- To practice extortion.[83]

One famous example of the word *exact* in the Bible involves John the Baptist. In Luke 3:13, John told tax collectors who asked him how to please God to *"Exact no more than that which is appointed you."* In other words, he instructed them not to tax subjects unfairly or steal from them using the taxation process. (Zacchaeus did this before he became a follower of Jesus.)

Many types of exactions tarnish governments today. Two common types that we've already reviewed include protective tariffs and inflation. Protective tariffs are unjust, because they rob *buyers* by taking away/raising the prices on cheaper foreign alternatives, while enriching *sellers* of that product. And inflation robs many individuals of the full value of their money, especially the poor, while enriching the politically connected, who get the new money first. But the curse of heavy taxation is nothing new. In fact, when Israel clamored for a king like other nations, God tried to get them to repent of this desire by warning them through the prophet Samuel what kings would do to the people:

> *"And he will take the tenth of your seed, and of your vineyards, and give to his officers, and to his servants. He will take the tenth of your sheep: and ye shall be his servants"* (1 Samuel 8:15, 17).

Imagine warning the people that their rulers would take *10 percent* of all they had! Most Americans today would *love* to drop to that tax percent. For example, "Tax Freedom Day" in America is typically in April (in 2019 it was on April 16). That is, the average American worked in that year all of January, February, March, and more than half of April...just to pay income, sales, property, vehicle, and other taxes.[84] That's about 30 percent of the year, or three times the amount that God warned the Israelites about!

But God didn't just command rulers, *"take away your exactions"* arbitrarily. Other than the fact that high taxes and unjust taxes irritate taxpayers, He had a good reason for forbidding exactions. In fact, God had *many* good reasons, long before perceptive economists discovered the negative effects of excess taxation upon economies. Let's look now at how excess taxes affect an economy, in a section titled...

How Excess Taxes Affect an Economy

Here are a few ways that excessive taxes affect an economy:

1. **They reduce employment.** When business owners look to expand, they almost always need to hire new employees. But when a new tax bill—or a higher *old* tax bill—stares them in the face, what are they

---

[83] *Webster's Dictionary 1828: American Dictionary of the English Language,* "Exaction," https://webstersdictionary1828.com/Dictionary/exaction.
[84] Erica York, Madison Mauro, Emma Wei, "Tax Freedom Day 2019 Is April 16th," April 20, 2019, Tax Foundation, https://taxfoundation.org/publications/tax-freedom-day.

supposed to do? They'll likely have to use the money they would have paid the new employee (or employees) to pay the tax instead.

2. **They slow down economic growth.** When taxes rise, millions of individuals save less money. This means less to invest in new technologies and inventions that do things like make shirts more cheaply, perform new lifesaving surgeries, increase computer speeds, grow fruits and vegetables more efficiently, and many more. All these delays or missed opportunities in investments retard economic progress and cost families wealth. In some cases, like when it involves medical care, it can even cost lives.

3. **They increase theft, fraud, and inefficiency.** Welfare is one glaring example of this. Back in 1989, in his book *Breaking the Poverty Cycle: Private Sector Alternatives to the Welfare State*, Robert Woodson found that "on average, 70 cents of each dollar budgeted for government assistance goes not to the poor, but to the members of the welfare bureaucracy and others serving the poor." Private charities, on the other hand, flipped that ratio.[85]

   And more than 15 percent of welfare programs are eaten up by fraud and abuse; in 2021 alone the total amount of welfare fraud in the U. S. was $161 billion.[86] Now, a little math: In 2020, there were 7.3 million families living "below the poverty line" in America.[87] If you divide $161 billion by 7.3 million, you get more than $22,000 given out fraudulently per family—not that every family gets that much more fraudulently, of course, but still! **To repeat: $22,000 isn't how much money is *spent* on welfare per family per year; that's the amount on average per family that is *stolen* from the welfare system per year.** *Every dollar that is spent by government bureaucrats, as we've already seen, is much more apt to be wasted or stolen than a dollar spent by workers who had to earn that money themselves.*

4. **They lower production.** Higher taxes discourage would-be entrepreneurs from starting new businesses. They discourage investors from investing, since the prospect of paying so much in taxes is disheartening, compared to the risk that investments will even pay off at all. And they discourage higher-income workers from working more hours and days, since those workers pay higher rates after they hit a higher income total. In fact, for over 100 years in this country a running joke has involved doctors taking many more days off (usually at the end of the year) to do things like play golf and go on vacation, instead of taking care of patients. It's based on reality, though—a reflection of those

---

[85] James Rolfe Edwards, "The Costs of Public Income Redistribution and Private Charity," *Journal of Libertarian Studies*, Summer 2007, Volume 21, No. 2, p. 4.
[86] "Welfare Fraud," Federal Safety Net, https://federalsafetynet.com/welfare-fraud.
[87] "Number of Families Living Below the Poverty Line in the United States from 1990 to 2021," *Statista*, statista.com/statistics/204743/number-of-poor-families-in-the-us.

doctors' frustrations and about having to pay such a giant percent of their income in taxes if they earned "too much money" that year. In the 1950s, when this joke perhaps reached its peak in popularity, the top income tax rate in the U. S., if a person made more than $200,000 per year, was *91 percent*.[88] You read that correctly. Henry Hazlitt expresses quite well the conundrum these high wage earners face:

> People begin to ask themselves why they should work six, eight, or ten months of the entire year for the government, and only six, four, or two months for themselves and their families. If they lose the whole dollar when they lose [if an investment fails], but can keep only a dime of it when they win, they decide that it is foolish to take risks with their capital.[89]

Visualize yourself working hard and sacrificing over many years to get to a certain income level.

Now, visualize only being allowed to keep only *nine percent* of what you made of that higher income!

Next, visualize the rest of that income taken away from you and used to pay for wasteful and immoral government programs—or to be handed over to others who didn't earn it—, instead of being used for food, clothing, or other items that *you* wanted to buy for yourself or your family.

Finally, visualize calm, soothing waves lapping up on the shore, so you won't be tempted to find the bureaucrat who thought up the 91 percent tax rate and punch him in the nose.

• • • • •

Unfortunately, partly because of the indoctrination of children, teenagers, and college students by many government schoolteachers, as well as ignorant (or untruthful) claims by media personalities who favor big-government policies, the number of Americans who believe that increased taxes benefit a nation's economy has exploded over the last few years.

But they're flat-out wrong.

Those persons might *think* high taxes are an overall benefit to society, because they can *see* the results right in front of them—for example, government workers building a $10 million structure by the side of the road.

But what those high-tax supporters *don't* see is the much greater good to the community—jobs, food, homes, inventions, and so on—that the same $10 million could have done if it were spent by *individuals*.

And those high-tax supporters don't think about how much more scrupulously those individuals would have spent their *own* money.

And those high-tax supporters don't think about how much of the $10 million spent on that government project is gobbled up by the enormous salaries

---

[88] "Historical U. S. Federal Individual Income Tax Rates & Brackets, 1862-2021," August 24, 2021, Tax Foundation, https://taxfoundation.org/historical-income-tax-rates-brackets.
[89] Hazlitt, *Economics in One Lesson*, 24.

of not the *workers*, but the *bureaucrats*—who, as we've already seen, make approximately twice what the average American makes.

Regardless of the corruption and injustice inherent in excessive taxes, not to mention how frustrating they are, Christians are still to pay them. As Paul instructs Christians in the book of Romans just a few verses down from saying rulers are to be a *"terror"* to *"evil,"* he says this:

> Render therefore to all their dues: tribute [personal and property taxes] to whom tribute is due; custom [other taxes] to whom custom; fear to whom fear; honor to whom honor (Romans 13:7).

Somehow, some way, despite a government's oppressive taxation, the Bible tells us in Philippians 4:19 that *"God shall supply all your need according to his riches in glory by Christ Jesus."*

What Do You Think?

1. Define the noun *exaction* and the verb *exact*.
2. Name two different forms of exactions. Explain why you would define each form as an exaction.
3. List several ways that cutting taxes would benefit a nation's economy.
4. A city government decides to tax every city resident to pay for a new football stadium. When some residents protest, the governor says, "You should be glad to pay this tax! The football games will bring in extra money to local businesses, which will benefit you and everyone else in our city." Is this an example of an *exaction*? Why or why not?
5. Quickly fill in the blanks:
   - "For no man ever yet ___ his own ___" (Ephesians 5:29).
   - "Let no man seek his ___, but every man ___" (1 Corinthians 10:24).
   - "Look not every man on his ___, but every man also on the ___" (Phillipians 2:4).

10.2 – CLAIM: "Saving Money Hurts the Economy!"

Today we analyze summaries of two news articles from 2009, just after an economic recession that began in 2008, brought about by destructive government policies. Both these articles express the same basic notion: that saving money—you guessed it!—*hurts the economy.*

• • • • •

Article 1: The first article comes from *Newsweek* magazine; its title is "To Save the Economy, We Need to Stop Saving." The article quotes (1) a bank Chief Executive Officer whose bank deposits "soared by nearly one third" during that recession, and (2) a pollster who found that twice as many Americans in that recession said they would save money, rather than invest it. The author asserts that to get out of the recession, Americans will have to spend more. In fact, he says Americans *must* increase their spending...

> Otherwise we fall into what economist John Maynard Keynes called the "paradox of thrift." If everyone saves during a slack period, economic activity will decrease, thus making everyone poorer.[90]

Article 2: The second article, titled "Hard-Hit Families Finally Start Saving, Aggravating Nation's Economic Woes," was published in the *Wall Street Journal* two months before the article mentioned above. This article describes two real-life families dealing with the recession by cutting their spending in various ways: shopping for clothes at thrift stores, eliminating trips to restaurants, keeping their old cars longer instead of buying new cars, buying fewer Christmas presents, and breeding pet hamsters for meat.

Okay, I guess *technically* those families didn't do that last thing. Everything else listed above they did, though. The article also points out that because of the recession, average American household debt *decreased* in 2008 for the first time in 56 years; many families cut their spending and increased their saving. The author of the article, Kelly Evans, then blames families who save more of their money for "failing stores, shuttered restaurants, and rising unemploy-

---

[90] Daniel Gross, "To Save the Economy, We Need to Stop Saving," *Newsweek*, March 13, 2009, newsweek.com/gross-save-economy-we-need-stop-saving-76561.

ment." She then declares, "Usually, frugality [thriftiness, economy] is good for individuals and the economy." Elsewhere in the article she says this, however:

> But this same thriftiness, embraced by families across the U. S., is also a major reason the downturn may not soon end. Americans, fresh off a decades-long buying spree, are finally saving more and spending less—just as the economy needs their dollars the most.[91]

• • • • •

With these article summaries in mind, and recalling what we've learned about economics so far, answer the questions that follow. (If you want, you may read the entire articles by going to the links at the bottom of those pages.)

What Do You Think?

1. Pretend you know nothing at all about economics. Does it sound right to you when an author or expert or economist claims that "When families save money, it's <u>bad</u> for the economy"? Why or why not?
2. In the middle of a recession or uncertainty about the future, why do individuals and families start saving more and spending less?
3. Define *interest rate*. What happens to the interest rate if there is an increase in savings? (Hint: What happens to the price of pickled beets if more pickled beets are available?)
4. How does the answer to the second part of Question #3 affect the amount of money that businesses borrow to buy new machinery or hire new employees?
5. Explain how economists who claim, "Saving is bad for the economy!" make one of the two basic mistakes that bad economists make. (This is the lesson of Bastiat's "What Is Seen, and What Is Not Seen.")
6. Why should we not be surprised when we hear some economists say things like "Saving is bad for the economy!"? (See Section 5.4 for a reminder.)

10.3 – Answering Economic Fallacies, Part 1

Read the following common assertions, which many often make today, and use what you've learned in Economics so far to answer them. Jot down your answers and bring them to our next class!

• • • • •

1. "I know some people out there think that we all should make all of our own buying and selling decisions, but most people just aren't that smart about economics. That's why we need to trust economic planners; it's a complicated subject, and only a few people really understand it well enough."

---

[91] Kelly Evans, "Hard-Hit Families Finally Start Saving, Aggravating Nation's Economic Woes," *The Wall Street Journal*, January 6, 2009, wsj.com/articles/ SB123120525879656021.

2. "The economy is struggling a lot right now, and some economists think we need the government to inject a little cash into our system, so we'll all be able to buy more. I totally agree; doing that will help the economy bounce back to where it needs to be."

3. "I oppose that new PublishPro printer and book binding machine, absolutely, 100 percent. Sure, maybe it *does* help individual writers publish books themselves; but it's going to throw a lot of publishing company employees out of work."

4. "The government needs to just open another public works program, because we're in a recession, and people need jobs. I mean, look over there at those guys building that bridge for the city! All of them are earning salaries that they use to buy things with; how can you possibly say that government spending *harms* the economy?"

10.4 – Not Very "Stimulating" At All • Quiz 7

Quickly review Section 8.3's "public works" reading; be sure you get Bastiat's main points! Then use the QR code to the right to be taken to a 2011 article which explains how jobs were supposedly created and saved by a bill passed by Congress and signed into law by then-President Barack Obama.

If your phone can't read that QR code, just search online for the article, using the key words or the link below.[92] (Or try teaching your phone a little phonics.)

Read the article, and answer the five below questions when you finish!

What Do You Think?

1. How much did this "stimulus" spending cost? How many jobs was it supposed to have created?

2. What was the average cost of each job the "stimulus" spending created if we assume the program actually did create the highest estimated number of 3.6 million jobs? How about the average cost if it created the lowest estimated number of 1.4 million jobs?

3. There were about 113 million full-time workers in the U. S. in 2011. Divide $821 billion by 113 million workers. How much did this "stimulus" program cost the average American worker?

4. Do you think the average American makes $228,055 to $586,428 per year? Look up the average salary of an American worker, then subtract that number

---

[92] Doug Mataconis, "2009 Stimulus Bill Cost $228,055 Per Job 'Saved or Created,'" Outside the Beltway, February 24, 2011, outsidethebeltway.com/2009-stimulus-bill-cost-228055-per-job-saved-or-created.

from $228,055. What figure did you get? Where do you think all this other money in the "stimulus bill" went?

5. Write as a single, short sentence what you think is this article's main lesson.

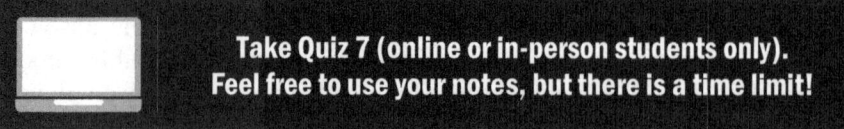

Take Quiz 7 (online or in-person students only).
Feel free to use your notes, but there is a time limit!

11.1 – The Minimum Wage Mess

In the U. S., as of 2022, the minimum hourly wage an employer is *allowed* to pay an employee is $7.25, an amount the U. S. government set in July 2009. (Some state laws impose a higher minimum wage than that.) Exceptions include farm workers, workers who receive tips, and golf caddies. The ways we can approach the subject of minimum wage are almost endless, but let's focus on a few.

Minimum Wage Law Realities

Government meddling in practically *all* areas of economics is objectionable, unjust, and harmful for the many reasons we've outlined in this book so far. But several specific reasons why governments shouldn't enact minimum wage laws are glaringly evident once we look at them:

1. **They're an improper use of power.** If we hold to the Bible's standards of the proper duties of government, we must conclude that they have no right to interfere with wages that employers and employees freely agree upon. On the other hand, should the government step in if an employer *cheats* (steals from) an employee, or vice versa? Absolutely! That's a perfect example of a government's responsibility to *"remove violence and spoil."* But the Bible is sensible about the limits of government duties by *omitting* the power to tell employers how much they must pay employees, since no government committee could possibly know how much the minimum wage "should" be.

   Legislators who claim to "know" what the new minimum wage ought to be are no different from planners who say they "know" better than buyers and sellers what the price of a can of pickled beets or a new laptop computer ought to be. *A wage is just a **price**—the price of the labor, knowledge, or skills that a worker sells to an employer.*

   And here's another monkey wrench to throw into the works: How can any legislator confidently say, "The proper minimum wage should be ___," when the cost of living in different areas of the country is so drastically different? In other words, if the national minimum wage were $10 per hour, someone making that much in New York City would be much worse off than a person making that in Wake Forest, North Carolina, for example. So...what's the magic formula to figure this out? Do we need teams of thousands—or *millions*—of bureaucrats going around calculating the cost-of-living differences in every U. S. city and town? And then figuring out the thousands of different minimum wage amounts in every location? And *continuing* to try to calculate it endlessly, since the cost of living will always keep changing?

Do you see how insane this idea of trying to determine the "correct" minimum wage is—and that, just like millions of buyers and sellers determine the price of oranges, they can also figure out the price of labor? (It's true that some *states* have higher minimum wages than the national law of $7.25, but the cost-of-living differences in numerous areas within those individual states can vary wildly.)

2. **They don't work, because of unintended consequences and the law of supply and demand.** Remember: A wage is a *price*. What happens to buyers when the price of gasoline increases? You know that they buy less of it. And the same thing happens when the price of labor—which is called a *wage*—increases. If an employer pays an unskilled or inexperienced worker $10 per hour because that employer has calculated that's what the employee's work is worth, and the minimum wage is raised to $15, what happens to that worker, and ones like him? *They will most likely lose their jobs, because the employer won't be able to afford them.* What's crazy is that this has been well known for decades! A 1978 survey, for example, showed that more than 90 percent of economists "agreed that the minimum wage increases unemployment among low-skilled workers."[93] But that didn't stop Congress in 2021 from considering the writing of a law forcing a $15-per-hour minimum wage across the country, even though Congress's own study estimated that *a $15-per-hour minimum wage would cause the loss of anywhere from 1.3 million to 3.7 million jobs!*[94]

Minimum wage supporters claim that we *must* raise wages, to help workers earn more. But if those supporters *really* believed their own policies, why stop at just $15 an hour? Why don't we raise the minimum wage to $50 or $100 or $1000 per hour? Wouldn't that make employees even richer? We can apply this logic to buying orange juice to show what would happen. What would happen if orange juice were $1000 per carton? Certainly, nearly everyone except the wealthiest and most orange-juice-obsessed buyers on earth would quit buying it. How about $100 per carton? Again, almost everyone would quit buying it—though not *quite* as many. The lower the cost of orange juice fell, the more consumers would buy it, although even at, say, $10 per carton, some who wanted orange juice still

---

[93] Linda Gorman, "Minimum Wages," Econlib: The Library of Economics and Liberty," econlib.org/library/Enc/MinimumWages.html.
[94] "The Effects on Employment and Family Income of Increasing the Minimum Wage," Congressional Budget Office, July 2019, cbo.gov/system/files/2019-07/CBO-55410-MinimumWage2019.pdf.

wouldn't be able to afford it. *And the same thing happens with forced wage increases*: Even at smaller increases, some employers—especially small businesses—won't be able to afford the product they're buying: the labor and skills of employees.

3. **They hurt those they're supposed to help.** Minimum wage increase advocates often claim, "It's only *fair* that employers pay their employees a *living wage*; nobody can make a good living working for today's minimum wage!" But as I might possibly have mentioned, government planners can't possibly know things like this. There's no way to precisely define a correct "living wage" for 100 million workers with different needs and living costs. (In fact, the absolute smartest group of planners that ever lived still couldn't manage these calculations correctly even if they tried to do it for 100 workers; I'd wager they couldn't even do it for 10.)

   And only about one to three percent of U. S. workers earn only the minimum wage anyway. They are almost always (a) young, (b) inexperienced, (c) lacking job skills, and (d) making more money before long.[95] By raising the minimum wage, however, the government torpedoes many low-level workers' situations. Instead of allowing an unskilled person to earn *some* money, produce wealth, and gain experience and self-respect, an increased minimum wage can result in that person's being laid off because he doesn't produce enough to make it worthwhile to his employer. Now that laid-off person makes *no* wages, and he produces *no* wealth.

4. **Early minimum wage laws were based on evolutionist racism.** When minimum wage laws were first instituted in the U. S. in the early 1900s, many leading supporters of these laws *knew* that they would increase unemployment among black and Chinese Americans.
   *And that's exactly **why** they supported those laws*
   The minimum wage law advocates' "inferior race" mindset led them to believe that black and Chinese Americans should be weeded out of society, partly by using minimum wage laws. Economist and minimum wage supporter John R. Commons (1862-1945) wrote this: "[Wage] competition has no respect for the superior races...The race with the lowest necessities displaces others." And Massachusetts Minimum Wage Commission member Arthur Holcombe bluntly admitted that the minimum wage laws enacted in Australia would "protect the white... standard of living from the invidious [unpleasant, offensive] competition of the colored races, particularly of the Chinese."[96]

   Does it logically follow that Christians should oppose minimum wage laws just because part of the reason they were brought into existence was a racist objective?

---

[95] "Characteristics of Minimum Wage Workers, 2017," Bureau of Labor Statistics, March 2018, bls.gov/opub/reports/minimum-wage/2017/home.htm.
[96] John Miltimore, "Seven Quotes That Reveal the Racist Origins of Minimum Wage Laws," Intellectual Takeout, August 28, 2019, https://intellectualtakeout.org/2019/08/seven-quotes-that-reveal-the-racist-origins-of-minimum-wage-laws.

No, but we can at least point out to others *why* minimum wage laws were originally pushed for. That fact ought to especially enlighten those who tend to blindly trust government, or those who believe that these laws came out of the pure, simple goodness of the hearts of those who just wanted to help their poorer fellow workers get a leg up.

Black Americans are still harmed by minimum wage laws today, especially young males who have disproportionately fewer job skills. This has zero to do with what shade of brown anybody is, obviously—it's a reflection of terrible government-run schools that graduate students with little hard or useful knowledge, as well as harmful consequences of government welfare programs that began destroying families in the 1960s. Economist Milton Friedman noted, "The people who have been hurt most by the minimum wage laws are blacks...[T]he most anti-black law on the books of this land is the minimum wage law."[97]

Milton Friedman

Minimum Wage Q&A

Don't employers usually take advantage of their employees by underpaying them and then making huge profits off their cheap labor?

Similar to how buyers and sellers *both* determine the price of goods and services like shoes, corn, eyeglasses, tires, and haircuts, employers (who are "buying" labor, skills, and knowledge) and employees (who are "selling" their labor, skills, and knowledge) *both* determine the price of of these. But let's say a business existed that was very profitable because its employees were paid unreasonably low wages. *Then* what would happen? Others would certainly get into that business to make similar profits, compete by paying *their* employees more, and force the original business to compete with higher employee pay. And the notion that most or nearly all employees are paid too low is an illogical myth. *A wage is just a name for the price of labor.* As Henry Hazlitt points out, those who claim that "labor is being 'underpaid' *generally*" would look ridiculous if they went around saying something like, "The prices of oranges and computers are *too low*!"[98]

But shouldn't employers treat their employees fairly?

Of course! Jesus followers should more than anybody. In fact, the Bible in several places addresses this very thing:

---

[97] Mark J. Perry, "Milton Friedman Responds to President Obama's Proposal to Raise the Minimum Wage Law, the Most "Anti-black Law in the Land," American Enterprise Institute, February 13, 2013, aei.org/carpe-diem/milton-friedman-responds-to-president-obamas-proposal-to-raise-the-minimum-wage-law-the-most-anti-black-law-in-the-land.
[98] Hazlitt, *Economics in One Lesson*, 124.

> "Woe unto him that buildeth his house by unrighteousness, and his chambers by wrong; that useth his neighbor's service without wages, and giveth him not for his work" (Jeremiah 22:13).
>
> "Thou shalt not defraud thy neighbor...the wages of him that is hired shall not abide with thee all night until the morning" (Leviticus 19:13).
>
> "...I will be a swift witness...against those that oppress the hireling in his wages, the widow, and the fatherless, and that turn aside the stranger from his right, and fear not me," saith the LORD of hosts (Malachi 3:5).
>
> Behold, the hire of the laborers who have reaped down your fields, which is of you kept back by fraud, crieth: and the cries of them which have reaped are entered into the ears of the Lord of sabaoth (James 5:4).

Fraud or theft, or what the Bible calls *spoil*, is certainly a matter for government intervention; an employee should get justice from an employer who steals wages from him. But a government committee has no idea what's "fair" to pay for this job or that job. Shouldn't two adults, or even an adult and a teenager, or possibly even an adult and an intelligent golden retriever, have the freedom to agree on what they think is a fair wage? Shouldn't an employer be free to pay what he wants using his own money, if the person whom he hires *freely agrees to it*?

How can governments help increase wages?

The same thing they can do to help the economy in other areas: *Get. Out. Of. The. Way.* A general truth on this subject is that **to increase your pay, increase your productivity**. In other words, if you want to be paid more, get more done, or get more accomplished!

We see this all the time in the real world. A car salesperson who sells more cars earns more. A pro basketball player who scores more points often gets a fat new contract. A bread maker using machines to make and slice more bread can sell more in a day. A carpenter using power tools produces more than one who uses hand tools. Those last two examples are significant: A key factor in increasing worker productivity is high-tech machines and other technology that ramp up the amount of goods that one person can produce. And as we've seen, when a government reduces taxes and business regulations, those businesses have more money to save and invest in new technologies and machines. To give another example, workers who use sewing machines, since they produce more than hand-sewers, get paid more. Here's how that works:

> The buyers [employers] do not pay for the toil and trouble the worker took, nor...the length of time he spent in working. They pay for the products. The better the tools are which the worker uses in his job, the more he can perform in an hour, the higher is, consequently, his [pay]. What makes wages rise...is improvement in the technological equipment. American wages are higher than wages in other countries because the capital invested...is greater, and the plants are thereby in the position to use the most efficient tools and machines.

> What is called "the American way of life" is the result of the fact that the United States has put fewer obstacles in the way of saving and capital accumulation than other nations. The economic backwardness of such countries as India consists precisely in the fact that their policies hinder both the accumulation of domestic capital and the investment of foreign capital. As the capital required is lacking, ...Indian enterprises are prevented from employing sufficient quantities of modern equipment, are therefore producing much less per manhour, and can only afford to pay wage rates which, compared with American wage rates, appear as shockingly low.
>
> There is only one way that leads to an improvement of the standard of living for the wage-earning masses...the increase in the amount of capital invested. All other methods, however popular...are not only futile, but are actually detrimental to the well-being of those they allegedly want to benefit.[99]

Workers who *produce* more get *paid* more. And machines and technology that help those workers produce more—and therefore earn more—multiply faster when governments don't tax the people half to death. Why? Because **increased taxation slows down the saving and investing that *pay* for individuals to invent, test, and produce those new machines.**

Two Final Thoughts

First, do you find it fishy that the same bureaucrats who claim they want to *help* the poor buy more by passing higher minimum wage laws...are the same ones who support inflation, which *decreases* the ability of the poor to buy more, since it devalues the money that they have?

Second, this section is a little longer than usual. Why? Because minimum wage laws are widely misunderstood by many. To the average person who doesn't understand economics (the subject is generally taught in government schools from a "The government should run the economy!" perspective), minimum wage laws *seem* to benefit the poor, when in fact they harm them—if not directly, then indirectly. And when critics of increasing the minimum wage *by the force of law* point out the flaws in doing that, you regularly hear conversations that sound something like this:

Bill: We should increase the minimum wage to $15 an hour; that'll help the poor buy more things.

Sam: If you wanted to help the poor buy more, and increasing the minimum wage really *worked*, why stop at $15 an hour? Why not increase it to $100 an hour, or even $1000 an hour?

Bill: Oh, come *on*! That's ridiculous, and you know it. You've got to raise it a *reasonable* amount for it to work, so employers don't lay off a lot of their workers.

---

[99] Ludwig von Mises, "Wages, Unemployment, and Inflation," *Christian Economics*, March 1958.

Sam: How about a $75-an-hour minimum wage? Or $50 an hour? Is that reasonable? Would employers lay off workers then?

Bill: Well...yeah, I'm sure they would; I think that's too much. You have to raise the minimum wage so employers can *afford* it.

Sam: $40 an hour? $30 an hour? $20 an hour? *What?*

Bill: Well...hmm...let's see...I think $20 an hour probably sounds pretty good. Yeah, I'd say employers could afford that.

Sam: *(Takes a deep breath and visualizes waves softly lapping up on the shore.)* How do *you* know that's the right amount employers should pay? Where's your *proof?* And what makes you think *anybody* or any *group* knows what that amount should be? Do you really think that bureaucrats could ever come to a definite conclusion that a certain dollar amount was the "correct" minimum wage they should *force* employers to pay? And since you agree that forcing employers to pay $100 an hour or $75 an hour would cause many of them to lay off employees, isn't it logical to assume that increasing the mini-mum wage to $40 or $30 or $20 an hour will *also* cause them to lay off employees, just not as many? And don't you realize that they'll lay off the workers making the *least*—the ones who most likely *really* need their jobs?

Bill: Well...I don't know, but come *on*! We've got to do *something*.

Sam: *(Punches Bill in the nose.)*

What Do You Think?

1. Why is a government official—or a group of government officials—unqualified to pronounce what the minimum wage should be?
2. What happens to workers at the lowest level when a higher minimum wage law is enacted? What is ironic about this occurrence?
3. Explain why the claim that "most workers are underpaid" is false.
4. How can workers increase their wages, and how can governments help them do so?
5. If you were an employer and the government raised the minimum wage you had to pay all your employees, and you gave employees free meals and a nice break room and bonuses, what might you do to make up the increased costs?

11.2 – Increasing Your Wages and Success at Work

After a chapter on the phenomenon of minimum wage laws—and the principle of wages themselves—, how can you approach the subject of *your* wages, and how to enjoy success at work?

Well, there are many ways. Here's a little advice based on a few experiences and observations.

Kicking "When Am I Ever Going to Use This?" Right in the Pants

First, if you're a student, approach your math, English, and other subjects with a little zest. Do your best to learn your math tables, fractions, decimals, percents, Algebra, and other math. Read your literature carefully. Write good drafts of papers you're asked to produce. Work, think, strive! And avoid using these common, lame excuses for turning in shoddy work:

- "I'm not a math person."
- "I'm right-brained."
- "I'm not a good writer."
- "I'm left-brained."
- "I was raised by goats."

And since you're a teenager, and you've probably been taught at home for much of—if not *all* of—your life, it's time to start taking ownership of your education. Mom and Dad or whoever is teaching you should have confidence that you'll do your work on your own, asking for help when you need it. It's incumbent upon you to make sure it gets done without having to be reminded all the time, like a toddler who keeps "forgetting" to pick up his toys!

On that note, it's certainly possible that you might come across a subject or which you think lacks any practical use. But even in that case, you should still

"When Am I Ever Gonna Use This Junk?"

avoid saying, "When am I ever going to *use* this?"—surely one of the most senseless utterances in the history of the world.[100]

Because the answer to that is, "You might not *ever* use what you're learning today, but you're learning it because, among other things, it's good practice in working hard." And it's also a lesson in humility, since when we're only teenagers, it's a little arrogant to assume that we know whether we'll ever use things we learn later in our lives. Case in point: John Saxon, the creator of Saxon Math, had a similar attitude about learning math when he was a young man, and he piddled his way through that subject in high school. Later, when he realized he wanted to be a pilot, he discovered that he had to learn or relearn

---

[100] just behind "**My** mask protects **you**, and **your** mask protects **me**!"

much of the math he could and should have done earlier, and his dream of flying took him longer than it would have otherwise.

Two more tips related to that subject:

First, you might think, *I just want to be a ___ for the rest of my life, and I don't need to learn ___ to do that.* But a new type of technology might take your job as a(n) ___ one day, and you could be stuck having to start a whole new career. And employers and customers are always looking for those who can help them solve problems. Struggling and sweating to write an effective essay and working out algebraic word problems, to name just two examples, are simply ways to practice problem-solving skills—even if you know you're never going to work as a writer or a mathematician.

Second, I can tell you from experience that gaining knowledge and skills from seemingly-pointless-at-the-time tasks happens regularly. I've been teaching English, math, and history high school homeschool classes since 2002, but I didn't start that as a career. (I never even knew it *was* a career until I got into it.) I had many jobs before where I wondered...

> *Why am I sitting here in this job? This isn't the kind of work I want to do for the rest of my life!*

"Why Do I Have to Read This Junk?"

This question popped up many times when in other jobs I had to learn things like photo editing, word processing, and spreadsheet software; database computer programs; customer service skills; the Saxon Math curriculum; newspaper article writing under tight deadlines; web site coding, and other duties that I thought were quite prosaic or had nothing to do with the type of work I thought I wanted to do. And I'm afraid that my attitude toward work wasn't what it should have been many times. Of course, I use all those skills now, but if someone had given me a choice at the time whether I had to learn them, I'd have been sorely tempted to say "No, thank you!" to a great many of them.

(In fact, when I was in school, my parents often made me read extra materials outside of my school readings, on various subjects such as math, politics, and economics, and I remember thinking at times, *Why do I have to **read** all this stuff?*)

Remember what the Lord tells us about how we approach the work He's given us:

> *The labor of the righteous tendeth to life (Proverbs 10:16a).*

> *And whatsoever ye do, do it heartily, as to the Lord, and not unto men; knowing that of the Lord ye shall receive the reward of the inheritance: for ye serve the Lord Christ (Colossians 3:23-24).*

Increasing Your Wages and Success at Work

Earnestly wanting to earn better wages isn't the same thing as slavishly pursuing riches, of course. That's why we can read in the Bible both *"[B]e content with your wages"* (Luke 3:14), John the Baptist's counsel to Roman soldiers who wanted to get right with God, as well as *"The workman is worthy of his meat,"* which Jesus said in Matthew 10:10 to his disciples who spread the gospel and were given to as they traveled. Part of the reason that Christians earn money, don't forget, is to *"support the weak"* (Acts 20:35). And do you remember how John Wesley encouraged Christians to earn all they can, save all they can, and give all they can? (See Section 2.3.)

As mentioned in the last section, when governments speed up saving and investing by reducing taxes and regulations, new technologies that make production faster appear more quickly. Workers increase their wages by increasing their *productivity* by using these machines and technologies. Those workers who make tables by hand, for example, receive wages, but workers who operate *machinery* that makes tables will receive more, because they *produce* more. And that benefits not just producers, but *buyers*—since machinery makes the cost of items like tables cheaper.[101]

At this point, you might not have many skills in operating high-tech machinery or computer technology, or other highly in-demand skills, so you might think, *How can I earn higher wages if I don't know much about that or have much experience?* The answer is:

You probably won't at first.

But that's not a problem; you're still young![102] And you *can* develop good work habits—start with cracking down on your math and writing, if necessary—and continue to learn about whatever work God puts in front of you. Aside from "hard workers," you should know that if you asked employers to describe the kind of employees they'd like to hire, they'd likely tell you that they're looking for those who have these skills or qualities:

1. They're willing to listen to and learn from those in the company with more experience and knowledge about how it works. If they have a question or suggestion, they ask or inform the appropriate person about it, without coming across as a know-it-all.

2. They don't demand their own way, but work with others and work toward the company's well-being—after all, its existence is the very reason why they have jobs!

---

[101] Hazlitt, *Economics in One Lesson*, 23-24.
[102] Unless your mom has flunked you repeatedly, and you're still being homeschooled at age 37! In which case you should consider running away from home! This afternoon!

3. They adhere to a key principle of professional propriety and maturity: totally shunning all gossip about and criticism of other employees, managers, or the company in general.

4. They work hard while maintaining this mindset: *If the company benefits, I have more of a chance to benefit too!*

5. They appreciate that the company's owner might have taken a huge risk by starting it; in fact, the owner might have risked his entire life savings, or even home, on that business. That owner also might have spent many nights without proper sleep because (a) he has worked very late doing jobs that needed to get done, or (b) he has often lain awake in bed thinking of ideas to help the business—maybe thinking of solutions to issues that came up. (And those employees realize that the owner is taking a risk by hiring *them*, too.[103])

I'm embarrassed to admit that I haven't, unfortunately, always followed this advice to a tee. In a few jobs I've had I got frustrated about some policy or boss or co-worker or all of the above, and I didn't live up to those expectations, not doing a good enough job for what I was being paid to do. But I've had a few successes trying to keep these points in mind. When I worked for a fast-food restaurant in high school, I did extra cleaning when I wasn't actively taking orders or making food, instead of just leaning on the counter doing as little as possible, like some employees did. And one of my managers noticed. Two years later, that manager and I happened to be in the same computer class at college; my academic advisor accidentally put me in that class, which was several levels too advanced! I struggled terribly with the work, but my old manager helped me for many hours, because he remembered when I tried to work hard at that restaurant.

Another job I had years later involved producing documents that were often hundreds of pages long. We paid a printer to create customized paper for these documents, but an idea occurred to me of how we could do it ourselves much more cheaply. The company that employed me started implementing my idea, saved tens of thousands of dollars per year, and gave me a nice raise.

Do a Good Job, Get Fired

But keep in mind: There's no guarantee that if you do good work, your boss or manager will praise you, or that you'll be handsomely rewarded with the riches of this life, like wads of cash and gold bars and chicken sandwiches with two pickles on them.

In fact, you might even irritate those around you *for doing a good job*! I was once fired from a writing/

---

[103] John Saxon risked his entire home to start his Saxon Math company; in fact, he even borrowed money from his own children to finance his idea! If his company had failed, he would have lost his home, after having paid tens of thousands of dollars on his mortgage for decades.

editing job; the manager came into my office a week after I received a good yearly evaluation (and a raise) and said, "We have to let you go. You're making too many spelling and punctuation errors," which was absolutely untrue. Another time I got a job doing simple accounting; the math was quite easy for me. But I avoided the gossip in the lunchroom, and many workers and managers had beliefs which I disagreed with (but without ever arguing or becoming confrontational). After this became known, one day my manager came into my office one day and said, "We have to let you go; you're making too many arithmetic mistakes," which was laughably false. And this kind of thing might happen to you, too! But don't worry:

> *But and if ye suffer for righteousness' sake, happy are ye: and be not afraid of their terror, neither be troubled; but sanctify the Lord God in your hearts: and be ready always to give an answer to every man that asketh you a reason of the hope that is in you with meekness and fear: Having a good conscience; that, whereas they speak evil of you, as of evildoers, they may be ashamed that falsely accuse your good conversation in Christ (1 Peter 3:14-16).*

Of course, the above passage refers more to Christians who suffered much more serious persecution for their faith than those who were only fired unjustly from their jobs, which pales in comparison to *real* persecution. But in a small way, the principle applies.

Men, Not Mules

To conclude this section, think about this: Part of the reason that Christians do what God tells us to do is simply because...that's what He tells us to do. This is, no doubt, a key reason why your parents or grandparents homeschool you—to teach you this important principle.

This principle starkly contrasts to the way most government schools generally train students all the way from kindergarten through high school, which is *not* that doing the right thing is its own reward. A significant percentage of government schoolteachers and administrators are disciples (whether they realize it or not) of John Dewey (1859-1952), perhaps *the* key figure—unfortunately—in American education history. As an atheist and a Marxist, Dewey believed that a school child was simply a higher evolved animal that teachers ought to train to behave in a certain way by offering rewards, like a farmer who dangles a carrot in front of a mule to get it to walk forward. Compare this belief to why a Christian obeys God—just to do the right thing for its own sake. And that's what we should do at our work.

So if you do well and are treated unfairly for it, don't let it bother you! A clear conscience before God is a precious thing. As Jesus says...

> *"Let your light so shine before men, that they may see your good works, and glorify your Father which is in heaven" (Matthew 5:16).*

> **What Do You Think?**

1. What's something very easy that a student could <u>look up</u> about a required subject or topic instead of whining, "When am I ever going to <u>use</u> this?"
2. What are some things you could do at your age to increase your knowledge and productivity, even if you don't have a great deal of experience with high-tech machinery or computers?
3. Look at the list of desirable employee characteristics. Have you ever been at a job or in a class with anyone who matches up—or <u>fails</u> to match up—with any of them? How did it affect your job or class?
4. How can Christians handle a situation in which they get unjustly fired or blamed for something? What can they do <u>beforehand</u> to make sure they have a good conscience in case it happens? Has this ever happened to you or to someone you know? Describe the situation.

11.3 – Labor Unions, Unequal Yoking, and Mammon

A Short Summary of Labor Unions

Striking Labor Union Members Battle Police

The following is a basic summary of labor unions in the U. S. These proliferated at the end of the nineteenth century, at which time workers in some industries banded together and threatened to walk out of their jobs all at the same time (this action is called a **strike**), partly to voice their disapproval of certain working conditions or pay grievances. Employers who faced a strike were often forced to either meet the striking workers' demands (often via orders of "union bosses"), or face potential financial ruin because their companies or factories produced nothing when union members remained on strike. Labor unions quickly became notorious for their corruption and violence. The extremely rewarding "union boss" positions—with access to millions of dollars in members' dues, as well as bribes from company representatives—were so highly sought after that many men who pursued those positions were brutally murdered by rivals.

Even though only about 10 percent of American workers belong to unions as of 2021,[104] their historical significance should certainly be mentioned. Here's a typical scenario that has played out hundreds of times—if not thousands—over the history of labor unions:

- Some workers at a company who do the same job (say, carpenters) are unhappy with their pay, their working conditions, or both.
- Many of those carpenters form a union. The carpenters who refuse to join the union are coaxed, harassed, threatened, and shunned by those who want *all* the company's carpenters to be union members.
- That union, through their "union boss," threatens the owner of the company with a strike unless its demands are met by a specific date. The company owner refuses to meet these demands, so the unionized carpenters go on strike.
- While the unionized carpenters are on strike, the non-union carpenters stay at work, and other carpenters not previously working for that employer are happy to take the now-unfilled jobs, as well as accept the pay and working conditions that union members rejected. These non-union carpenters and new workers are called **strike-breakers**; the workers they replace often call them "scabs."
- In retaliation, the carpenter labor union boss threatens the strike-breakers. Some are afraid, so they quit. Some do not quit, however, and they pay a price: Their tires are slashed, they are beaten by union thugs, and their wives receive threatening (anonymous) phone calls. Some strikebreakers' homes are firebombed, and some are even murdered, to send a message to remaining strikebreakers.
- The owner of the company of which the carpenters' union has essentially taken over gives in and pays the carpenters the higher wage, and/or meets other demands. To keep from losing money, he is forced to raise prices on his products.

The negative effects of this kind of thing are numerous, but let's just focus on a few.

First, labor unions typically visualize workers in the same profession as one giant lump, instead of as distinct individuals. We have already learned how workers are generally paid based on their *production* (although this is an imperfect process, of course). This raises the question: Why should one member of that carpenters' union, for example, make the same wage as another member of the union who is *more* productive? Or why should all members of that union (or any union) get raises, when they don't all *deserve* to get raises?

And how do you think union members feel about non-union members who produce more than they do? It isn't too hard to deduce that the atmosphere in

---

[104] "Union Members – 2021," Bureau of Labor Statistics, January 20, 2022, bls.gov/news.release/pdf/union2.pdf.

such workplaces can get to be so tense and discordant that it becomes difficult for those two groups to work together at all.

Second, since the company owner must raise his prices to cover the higher cost of labor after a successful union strike, this forces customers to either pay higher prices, buy less, or do without the item that the company produces. Fewer buyers mean ill effects for those union members, and the owner will be less likely to hire more workers or invest in new machines. And what if more unions form and do the same thing? It only results in higher prices on many other goods and services (which is already happening, incidentally), and any gains made by those unions are in effect lost to the higher prices of items they eventually have to pay on items made by other unions. In other words, it's ridiculous to celebrate a wage increase your union boss gets for you, if that increase ends up barely buying what it used to because of resulting price increases of goods and services.

Pro-Union Poster

Third, for many decades the U. S. government has heavily favored labor unions over company owners—often called "management." The National Labor Relations Board, a government bureaucracy created in 1935 under President Franklin D. Roosevelt, often stepped in—unconstitutionally, by the way—to settle many labor vs. management disputes in various industries. Management was blamed for an overwhelming percentage of the disputes, which is no surprise, since many of the officials in Roosevelt's administration favored forms of socialism/fascism. Many government officials who meddle in labor vs. management disputes even today strongly believe the Marxist idea that management is made up of nothing but bad guys who exploit poor workers, so those officials think something like this:

> *It would be much better for everyone to live under a glorious,* **glorious** *system of socialism or communism. But if that isn't possible yet, at least we government officials can help the workers slaving under the greedy and evil capitalists. If we government saviors don't, those poor workers*

will surely be sent to Mordor to work in salt mines and given nothing but dirty water and moldy bread crusts to live on.

America's largest, most powerful union is a teachers' union: The National Education Association. When I worked one year as a government school math teacher, the union representatives hounded me to join, but I refused. The union (like many other teachers' unions) had arranged a setup so that teachers would make more money every additional year they had taught school—regardless of how effective they were. When I realized that, I thought, *Why should some teachers make more just because they've been in the school system longer? Shouldn't higher pay be based on **merit**?*

Also, it's well known that membership in a teachers' union can act as a shield for rotten or even borderline criminal teachers. Some teachers, administrators, and assistant principals I saw in the high school in which I worked were so lazy and/or incompetent that I couldn't *believe* they had jobs. But their membership in the teachers' union went a long way to protect them from scrutiny. In fact, in some teachers' unions contracts make it so it costs the state hundreds of thousands of dollars and *years* of effort to fire even *one* rotten or incompetent teacher, so the schools often do nothing.

Important Note: As a balance, it must be acknowledged that employers often share the blame in many disputes with employees. Some companies' owners and/or managers have treated employees unfairly, cheated them out of wages, and/or unjustly fired them if they asked for better working conditions—instead of listening to reasonable concerns. A reminder: Owners, managers, *and* employees are all humans; they're self-seeking and sinful!

Two Final Questions

Christians can be faced with the decision of whether they should join a labor union. I don't want to make any dogmatic statements, but it's helpful to keep a few biblical admonitions in mind:

> *Servants, be obedient to them that are your masters according to the flesh, with fear and trembling, in singleness of your heart, as unto Christ; not with eyeservice, as menpleasers; but as the servants of Christ, doing the will of God from the heart; with good will doing service, as to the Lord, and not to men (Ephesians 6:5-7).*

> *Be ye not unequally yoked together with unbelievers: for what fellowship hath righteousness with unrighteousness? And what communion hath light with darkness? (2 Corinthians 6:14).*

> *"No man can serve two masters: for either he will hate the one, and love the other; or else he will hold to the one, and despise the other. Ye cannot serve God and mammon* [riches]*" (Jesus, Matthew 6:24).*

> *"The workman is worthy of his meat" (Jesus, Matthew 10:10).*

Two questions, then, that we'll end with: (1) Should Christians join labor unions?; and (2) should Christians look at themselves as only members of a group of workers, instead of individuals whose wages or income should be based on how well they do their jobs?

> **What Do You Think?**
>
> 1. What basic mistake in economic thinking do labor unions make when they focus only getting more for their members? Why is this mistake easy to understand, given what we know about man's nature?
> 2. Do you think union membership leads an individual to try to produce more, less, or the same? Why?
> 3. List some reasons why Christians should carefully consider whether to join a labor union.

11.4 – "Unintended Consequences," Part 2 • Quiz 8

Today, let's try another few rounds of **Unintended Consequences!** Try to deduce what unintended consequences followed these government economic policies. (We'll talk about the cases in our next class.)

• • • • •

Unintended Consequence 1: Let's Tax and Regulate Vaping! Alarmed by the increased use of electronic nicotine delivery systems (or ENDS, commonly called "vaping") among 18-25-year-olds, more than half of state governments in the U. S. impose taxes and other regulations upon them. These additional taxes are intended to reduce the practice of vaping and the damaging health effects it causes among those who do it. Because of the now-higher cost of ENDS, what do you think many vapers in that age range now do instead of vaping?[105]

Unintended Consequence 2: Student Loans. In 1965, Congress passes the Higher Education Act, which includes the Guaranteed Student Loan program, promising those who lend money to students to pay for college educations that the U. S. Government will repay them if students fail to pay back the loans. The government has been involved in other ways too, including reducing the interest rates on stu-

---

[105] Abigail S. Friedman, Michael F. Pesko, "Young Adult Responses to Taxes on Cigarettes and Electronic Nicotine Delivery Systems," Wiley Online Library, July 19, 2022, https://onlinelibrary.wiley.com/doi/full/10.1111/add.16002.

dent loans. What unintended consequences do you think result?[106]

Unintended Consequence 3: Let's End Poverty! In 1965, the U. S. government embarks upon what they refer to as the "War on Poverty." The program expands over decades to include various components: cash payments to welfare recipients, food stamps/coupons,  free medical care, and aid to unwed mothers. What do you think happens to the number of single-parent families after the War on Poverty, and why?[107]

 **Take Quiz 8 (online or in-person students only). Feel free to use your notes, but there is a time limit!**

12.1 – Test 4

If you're in my in-person or online Economics class, take Test 4 today. This test focuses on material from Weeks 9-11, but also might contain material from previous weeks. First review your notes, then take Test 4!

12.2 – CLAIM: "Statistics <u>Prove</u> That Socialism Works!"

Fill in the blanks of the below verses from memory, which discuss the legitimate purposes of government:

- To *"[R]emove ___ and ___, and execute ___ and ___"* (Ezekiel 45:9)
- To *"Deliver the ___ out of the hand of the oppressor"* (Jeremiah 22:3)
- To punish *"___"* (1 Peter 2:13-14)
- To be a *"terror"* and *"revenger"* to *"___"* (Romans 13:4)

---

[106] Veronique de Rugy, "Subsidized Loans Drive College Tuition, Student Debt to Record Levels," *Washington Examiner*, July 12, 2013, washingtonexaminer.com/subsidized-loans-drive-college-tuition-student-debt-to-record-levels

[107] Sam Jacobs, "Black America Before LBJ: How the Welfare State Inadvertently Helped Ruin Black Communities," The Burning Platform, January 9, 2020, theburningplatform.com/2020/01/09/black-america-before-lbj-how-the-welfare-state-inadvertently-helped-ruin-black-communities.

Now, on to our scenario for today:

The Scenario: You're sitting at a fast-food restaurant, enjoying a chicken sandwich (with two pickles on it) and some waffle fries. After eating for a few minutes, you suddenly get a strange feeling that you're being watched. You whirl around quickly, and there he is again: your economics college professor, standing right behind you. He says this:

> People who are against socialism are either biased against it, or they just don't know what they're talking about. Dr. Julie Casper, the respected historian and author, discovered that socialism improved the economy by 47 percent in the nation of Kliftonia under the leadership of Queen Melodia Anna VIII. And that's not all: Five other poorer nations from 1993-2014 converted to socialistic economies and experienced *incredible* growth. Given that, how can anyone *possibly* oppose socialism? (Now give me some of your waffle fries.)

How could you respond to your professor's claim? (Hint: Don't worry if you don't know much about statistics or individual nations' economies; just remember what you know about socialism and man's nature.) Jot down a few ideas in your economics notebook.

12.3 – CLAIM: "The Government Has to Build Roads!"

55 Million and Counting

One obvious, common, and frustrating evidence of government inefficiency and waste and poor quality is the system of roads. We've all driven on—and been driven a little crazy by—badly marked and poorly lighted state roads.

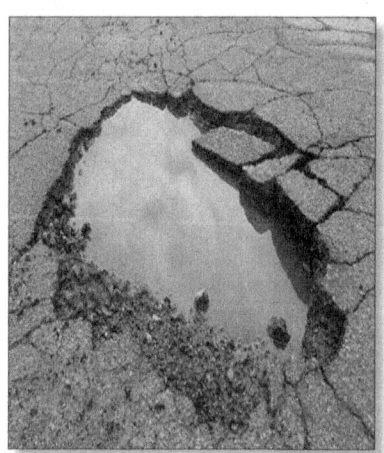

And *potholes*? I could write an entire *book* on potholes. (It would be boring, but I could write it.) On some roads that I drive on regularly, I find that my hands almost instinctively swerve my car around potholes, without my even having to concentrate on avoiding them. Why?

That's easy: It's because I have *memorized* where those numerous potholes are, given that they've been there since, approximately, the American Revolution. And even if one of those potholes *is* finally filled, it's almost never filled *smoothly*. When my tires run over a used-to-be pothole that has *finally* been filled—too full, of course—, it often gives me a nice little jolt in my spine, like I'm running over a small dog.[108]

About 30 minutes from where I live, a person can drive around an extensive area that contains many beautiful, multimillion-dollar homes. And the exquisite landscaping and luxurious features of these estates are beautifully enhanced by surrounding state roads that look like they've been bombed by a horde of invading Martians.

Government-built, government-repaired roads (state or federal roads; it really doesn't matter which) are so universally recognized as terrible that a joke about them has been around for decades:

Q: What are the two main types of roads?

A: Those that are *being* fixed, and those that *need* to be fixed.

Hilarious.

But wretched roads are more than just a simple nuisance; they're potentially deadly to those drivers and passengers who use them regularly. Here's an astounding fact: Approximately 55 *million* potholes plague "public" roads in the U. S.[109] In fact, back in 2015, the American Society of Civil Engineers estimated that badly maintained roads within the United States cost Americans more than $100 *billion* (not *million*) per year.[110] Even worse, government roads can *kill* drivers and others. From 2018 to 2020, for example, car crashes caused by potholes killed more than 5,600 individuals in India, according to that nation's own government study.[111]

A Terrifying Idea?

Even though it's *totally obvious* to anybody who is even half conscious that state roads inconvenience, endanger, injure, and even *kill* travelers, when supporters of limited government and a voluntarily cooperating economy suggest that *private* companies owned by and working with individuals should take charge of the roads, critics often react something like this:

> Wait a minute, now, *WAAAIT* just a minute! Okay, I guess it's true that free markets work in *most* situations to make goods and services available to customers, but not *all* situations! I mean, **what about the roads**?! You can't just let the *market* do *that*! People would just stop everybody else from driving by their houses; traffic lights and stop signs wouldn't even *exist*! And even if they did, people would charge us big bucks just to drive down the street to the grocery store!

---

[108] A cute little Yorkshire Terrier puppy, for example.
[109] "How Many Accidents Are Caused by Potholes Each Year?", Sage-Advices, August 21, 2020, https://sage-advices.com/how-many-accidents-are-caused-by-potholes-each-year.
[110] John W. Schoen, "Bad Roads Cost Car Owners Billions: Report," CNBC, July 23, 2015, cnbc.com/2015/07/23/bad-roads-cost-car-owners-billions-report.html.
[111] "Road Accidents Caused by Potholes Killed Over 5,600 People Between 2018 and 2020," *Deccan Herald*, August 22, 2022, deccanherald.com/national/road-accidents-caused-by-potholes-killed-over-5600-people-between-2018-and-2020-1138292.html.

With that claim in mind, brainstorm one or two solutions on what *you* would do to allow the free market to take care of the road challenge if the government announced it would no longer build, repair, or otherwise maintain any roads. **Write these down and bring them to class next week.** Note: These don't have to be comprehensive, detailed plans—just some ideas that might contribute toward solving the issue.

One thought you might want to keep in mind: The U. S. government and state governments add taxes to every gallon of gas purchased; this money is supposed to go toward building and fixing roads. About how much extra money per gallon do gas customers in your state pay for this? (Look it up before you start your brainstorming!)

Go ahead and brainstorm and write down your solutions!

12.4 – "The Rich and the Poor: A Fairy Tale"

"The Rich and the Poor: A Fairy Tale" is a fascinating, instructive little story that comes from *John Hopkins's Notions on Political Economy*, a collection of economic essays published in 1833 by English political and science writer Jane Marcet (1769-1858).

• • • • •

In the time of the Fairies, things went on no better than they do at present. John Hopkins, a poor laborer, who had a large family of children to support upon very scanty wages, applied to a Fairy for assistance. "Here am I half starving," said he, "while my landlord rides about in a fine carriage; his children are pampered with the most dainty fare, and even his servants are bedizened with gaudy liveries:[112] in a word, rich men, by their extravagance, deprive us poor men of bread. In order to gratify *them* with luxuries, *we* are debarred almost the necessaries of life." "'Tis a pitiable case, honest friend," replied the Fairy, "and I am ready to do all in my power to assist you and your distressed friends. Shall I, by a stroke of my wand, destroy all the handsome equipages, fine clothes, and dainty dishes, which offend you?" "Since you are so very obliging," said honest John, in the joy of his heart, "it would perhaps be better to destroy all luxuries whatever: for, if you

Jane Marcet

---

[112] "bedizened with gaudy liveries": decorated with fancy uniforms

confine yourself to those you mention, the rich would soon have recourse to others; and it will scarcely cost you more than an additional stroke of your wand to do the business outright, and get rid of the evil root and branch."

No sooner said than done. The good-natured Fairy waved her all-powerful wand, and, wonderful to behold! the superb mansion of the landlord shrank beneath its stroke, and was reduced to a humble thatched cottage. The gay colors and delicate textures of the apparel of its inhabitants faded and thickened, and were transformed into the most ordinary clothing; the greenhouse plants sprouted out cabbages, and the pinery[113] produced potatoes. A similar change took place in the stables and coach-house: the elegant landau[114] was seen varying in form, and enlarging in dimensions, till it became a wagon; while the smart gig shrunk and thickened into a plough. The manes of the horses grew coarse and shaggy, their coats lost all brilliancy and softness, and their legs became thick and clumsy: in a word, they were adapted to the new vehicles they were henceforward to draw.

Honest John was profuse in his thanks, but the Fairy stopped him short. "Return to me at the end of the week," said she; "it will be time enough for you to express your gratitude when you can judge how much reason you have to be obliged to me."

Delighted with his success, and eager to communicate the happy tidings to his wife and family, John returned home. "I shall no longer," said he to himself, "be disgusted with the contrast of the rich and the poor: what *they* lose must be our gain, and we shall see whether things will not now go on in a different manner." His wife, however, did not receive him with equal satisfaction; for, on having gone to dress herself (it being Sunday) in her best cotton gown, she beheld it changed to a homely stuff; and her China tea-pot, given her by her landlord's wife, and on which she set no small store, though the handle was broken, was converted into crockery ware!

She came with a woeful countenance[115] to communicate these sad tidings to her husband. John hemmed and hawed, and at length wisely determined to keep his own counsel, instead of boasting of being the author of the changes which had taken place. Presently his little boy came in crying. "What ails you, Tommy?" said the father, half pettishly, and somewhat suspecting that he might have caused his tears also. "Why, daddy," replied the urchin, "as I was playing at battledore[116] with Dick, the shuttlecock flew away and was lost, and the battledores turned into two dry sticks, good for nothing but to be burnt." "Psha!" cried the father, who was beginning to doubt whether he had not done a foolish thing. In order to take time to turn over the subject in his mind, and console himself for his disappointment, he called for his pipe. The good wife ran to fetch it, when, lo and behold! the pipes were all dissolved! There was pipe-clay in plenty, but no means of smoking. Poor John could not refrain from

---

[113] greenhouse for growing pineapples
[114] horse and carriage
[115] expression
[116] badminton

an oath, and, in order to pacify him, his wife kindly offered him a pinch of snuff. He took the box: it felt light, and his mind misgave him as he tapped it. It was with too much cause; for, on opening it, he found it empty! At length, being alone, he gave vent to his vexation and disappointment. "I was a fool," cried he, "not to desire the Fairy to meddle with the luxuries of the rich only. We have so few, that it is very hard we should be deprived of them. I will return to her at the end of the week, and beg her to make an exception in our favor." This thought consoled for awhile; but, long before the end of the week, poor John had abundance of cause to repent of all he had done. His brother Richard, who was engaged in a silk manufactory, was, with all the other weavers, turned out of work. The silk had disappeared; the manufacturers, with ruin staring them in the face, had sent their workmen out upon the wide world. Poor John, conscience-struck, received his starving brother into his house. "You will see great changes for the better soon," said he, "and get plenty of work." "Where and how?" cried Richard. But that was more than John would say.

Soon after, Jack, his eldest son, returned home from the coach-maker with whom he worked; all the carriages being changed into wagons, carts, and ploughs. "But why not remain with your master, and work at the carts instead of the coaches?" said his father. "Nay, but he would not keep me, he had no work for me; he had more carts and wagons than he could dispose of for many a day: the farmers, he said, had more than they wanted, and the cartwright business was at an end, as well as coachmaking."

John sighed; indeed, he well-nigh groaned with compunction.[117] "It is, however, fortunate for me," said he, "that I earn my livelihood as a laborer in the fields. Corn and hay, thank God! are not luxuries; and I, at least, shall not be thrown out of work."

In a few days, however, the landlord, on whose estate he worked, walked into the cottage. John did not immediately know him, so much was his appearance altered by a bob wig, a russet suit of clothes, and worsted stockings. "John," said he, "you are an honest hard-working man, and I should be sorry you should come to distress. Here are a couple of guineas,[118] to help you on till you can find some new employment, for I have no further occasion for your services." John's countenance, which had brightened up at the sight of the gold, now fell most heavily. He half suspected that his landlord might have discovered the author of all the mischief (for such he could no longer conceal from himself that the change really was), and he muttered, that "he hoped he had not offended his honor?" "Do not *honor* me: we are all now, methinks, peasants alike. I have the good fortune, however, to retain my land, since that is not a

---

[117] regret
[118] English coins

luxury; but the farm is so much larger than, in my present style of living, I have any occasion for, that I mean to turn the greater part of it into a sheep-walk, or let it remain uncultivated." "Bless your honor, that would be a sad pity! Such fine meadows, and such corn! But cannot you sell the produce, as before? for corn and hay are not luxuries." "True," replied the landlord, "but I am now living on the produce of less than half my estate; and why take the trouble to cultivate more? for since there are no luxuries to purchase, I want no more money than to pay my laborers, and buy the homely clothes I and my family are now obliged to wear. Half the produce of my land will be quite sufficient for these purposes."

Poor John was now reduced to despair. The cries of distress from people thrown out of work everywhere assailed his ears. He knew not where to hide his shame and mortification till the eventful week had expired, when he hastened to the Fairy, threw himself on his knees, and implored her to reverse the fatal decree, and to bring back things to what they had been be-fore. The light wand once more waved in the air, but in a direction opposite to that in which it before moved; and immediately the stately mansion rose from the lowly cottage; the heavy teams began to prance and snort, and shook their clumsy harness till they became elegant trappings: but most of all was it delightful to see the turned-off workmen running to their looms and their spindles; the young girls and old women enchanted to regain possession of their lost lace-cushions, on which they depended for a livelihood; and every thing offering a prospect of wealth and happiness, compared to the week of misery they had passed through.

John grew wise by this lesson; and, whenever anyone complained of the hardness of the times, and laid it to the score of the expenses of the rich, took upon him to prove that the poor were gainers, not losers, by luxuries; and when argument failed to convince his hearers, he related his wonderful tale. One night at the public house, Bob Scarecrow, who was one of the listeners, cried out, "Ay, it is all fine talk, folks being turned out of work if there were no luxuries; but for his part, he knew it, to his cost, that he at least lost *his* livelihood because his master spent his all in luxuries. The young lord whom he served as gamekeeper set no bounds to his extravagance, until he had not a farthing left; and then his huntsmen, his hounds, his gamekeeper, and his laced livery-servants, were all sent off together! Now, I should be glad to know, honest John," added Bob, "whether *we* lost our places because there was too much luxury, or too little?" John felt that there was some truth in what Bob said; but he was unwilling to give up the point. At length a bright thought struck him, and he triumphantly exclaimed, "Too *few,* Bob! why, don't you see, that as long as your master spent his money too freely in luxuries, you kept your places, and when he was ruined and spent no more, you were turned off?"

Bob, who was a sharp fellow, saw the weakness of John's argument, and replied, "that it was neither more nor less than a quibble, fit for a pettifogging[119] lawyer; for," said he, "suppose that every man of substance were to spend his all, and come to ruin, a pretty plight we poor folks should be in: and you can't deny, that, if the rich lived with prudence, and spent only what they could afford, they would continue to keep us in employment." John felt convinced; and he was above disowning it. "I grant you," said he, "that there may be too much luxury as well as too little, as was the case with your young lord. But then you must allow, that if a man don't spend more than he can afford, that is, if he don't injure *himself, we* have no reason to complain of his luxuries, whatever they may be, because they give us work, and that not for a short time, after which we are turned off, as was your case, but regularly and for a continuance."

John now went home, satisfied that the expenses of the rich could not harm the poor, unless the expenses first injured the rich themselves. No bad safeguard, thought he; and as he trudged on, pondering it in his mind, he came to this conclusion:

"Why then, after all, the rich and the poor have but one and the same interest—that is very strange! I always thought they had been as wide apart as the east is from the west! But now I am convinced that the comforts of the poor are derived from the riches of the rich."

What Do You Think?

1. What early evidence is there that John won't benefit from his wish?
2. In what negative ways do John's wish affect even the poor?
3. How is the story's moral expressed at the end?
4. Give a modern example of how the story's last line is true.

13.1 – "Unintended Consequences," Part 3

You guessed it: It's time for another round of *Unintended Consequences*. Once again, try to figure out what unintended consequences might follow the following three government acts and policies. Be sure to especially use what you know about man's nature to help you predict these scenarios' outcomes.

Case 1: The Eyes Don't Have It. Millions of residents of the (very young) nation of Kliftonia suffer from poor eyesight. But wait...carrots are great for eyesight, aren't they? Even little kids know that carrots are rich in Vitamin A...or maybe it's Vitamin D, or Potassium, or Magnesium, or Uranium, or something. At any rate, high-level bureaucrats announce that Kliftonia's government will pay farmers—

---

[119] unimportant

and anybody else, for that matter—to grow carrots—in fact, it will pay carrot growers *twice* the price that they usually receive. Can you think of some of the unintended consequences that might occur in this scenario?

Case 2: Longer Unemployment Benefits. Because of government economic policies, including an ill-advised decision to pay growers twice the market price for carrots, the job market is terrible in Kliftonia. Even though those laid off or fired from their jobs normally receive unemployment payments for six weeks, Kliftonia's Department of Labor announces that it will double unemployment payments to 12 weeks. What unintended consequences do you think could happen due to this policy?

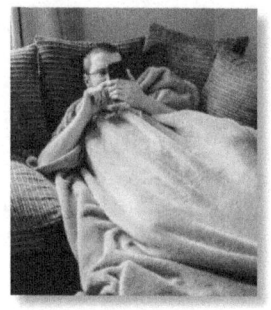

Case 3: COVID-19 Bonus Money. Okay, let's head back to the U. S. for this real-life scenario. Medicare, a system of government-run and taxpayer-funded health care for senior citizens, pays doctors to treat patients. In 2020, U. S. lawmakers announce that there is a health "pandemic," *and* they change Medicare policy so that doctors are paid *20 percent more* to treat those patients who are said to "test positive for COVID-19." What unintended consequences do you think might occur in this scenario?[120]

13.2 – Answering Economic Fallacies, Part 2

Read the following five common economic fallacies—ones we have discussed previously—which many believe today. Use what you've learned in this book so far to answer these claims. (Don't forget to think about these concepts: What is the proper purpose of government? What is mankind's nature? What are potential unintended consequences of government actions?) Jot down your answers, and if you're in my in-person or online class, bring them so we can discuss them!

• • • • •

1. "The government should arrest and throw in jail all those price gougers who charge too much for batteries, gasoline, bottled water, and other items that people are going to need during the coming

---

[120] Rich Daly, "Increased Medicare Payments for COVID-19 Care To Stretch Back to Late January," Healthcare Financial Management Association, April 21, 2020, hfma.org.topics/news/2020/04/increased-medicare-payments-for-covid-19-care-to-stretch-back-to.html.

hurricane. I'm so tired of their being allowed to jack up their prices when people need those items the most. That's not fair at all!"

2. "It would be better to live under a system of socialism run by the government, instead of under capitalism. Socialism is a more equal structure, since under capitalism employers underpay workers, hurt the poor, and think about nothing except getting rich."

3. "We need to put tariffs on bubble gum imported from Kliftonistan. Our nation's top bubble gum manufacturers are losing business right and left, because our country is being flooded with cheap foreign bubble gum."

4. "The Federal Reserve should decide what interest rates that banks are allowed to charge borrowers. Those who work at the Fed are specialists, and without their guidance, money lenders would charge borrowers too high of an interest rate, which would hurt the economy."

5. "Of course, I'm not *glad* about the destruction and killing that happened during World War II, but it *did* help finally end the Great Depression! During the war, millions of Americans were put to work making machine guns, bombs, and planes, and millions of men got jobs as soldiers. It really ended up boosting the economy."

13.3 – "The Luxury Tax Myth"

Today you'll read "The Luxury Tax Myth,"[121] an article by Bill Yeargin, President and CEO of Correct Craft, a company that manufactures boating products in several U. S. locations. (You can access this article by scanning the QR code to the right or visiting the link at the bottom of the page.) In that article, Yeargin addresses not only the effects of taxing so-called "luxury" items like boats, but the effects of government attempts to "soak the rich," so politicians can raise money to spend, *and* even claim that they're "helping the poor." After you read the article, answer the review questions below.

What Do You Think?

1. Why does Yeargin say that luxury taxes, like the ones on boats, are perfect examples of "unintended consequences"? →

---

[121] Bill Yeargin, "The Luxury Tax Myth," Boating Industry, February 2, 2022, https://boatingindustry.com/blogs/2022/02/01/the-luxury-tax-myth.

2. **Sum up the disastrous 1990 "luxury tax" on boats.**
3. **In what way did the boat buyers act after that tax was enacted—a reaction that Congress didn't predict?**
4. **Why do you suppose that obvious lessons, like the one about luxury taxes, are rarely learned by legislators?**

13.4 – CLAIM: "College Should Be <u>Free</u>!" • Quiz 9

Later in today's section, we'll look at how we can answer a claim about governments and college. First, as much as you can from memory, fill in the blanks of the below four verses that sum up the Biblical, true purpose of government:

- To *"remove ___ and ___, and execute ___ and ___"* (Ezekiel 45:9)
- To *"deliver the ___ out of the hand of the ___"* (Jeremiah 22:3)
- To punish *"___"* (1 Peter 2:13-14)
- To be a *"terror"* and *"revenger"* to *"___"* (Romans 13:4)

• • • • •

The Scenario: It's exactly noon on a beautiful, clear, crisp Thanksgiving Day, and you're looking forward to a wonderful celebration, since many of your favorite relatives have come over to enjoy a bountiful Thanksgiving meal. Everybody is gathered around the table, but right then your doorbell rings unexpectedly.

Who in the world could it be?

When you open the door, you see—surprise, surprise!—your economics professor, who wants to lecture you about yet another economic dogma he believes. You happily accept his invitation; in fact, you even invite him in to share your thanksgiving meal. Unfortunately, he runs away, screaming that eating turkey "causes climate change."

• • • • •

It's now three hours later, and you and your second cousin have managed to stagger from the dining table, eventually collapsing on two living room recliners, nearly unable to move after having pounded down approximately a third of your entire body weights in turkey, mashed potatoes, green beans, pickled beets, and three types of pies (with gravy). Then, with a great effort and a loud grunt of discomfort, your second cousin manages to roll himself over so that he's facing you. After another grunt, he takes a deep breath, then mumbles this in your direction:

> You know, our state government should just pay for degrees for all the students going to colleges or universities in our state. I mean, it makes sense, because college degrees make graduates more valuable as em-

ployees, and that benefits the economy. And it's not like our state can't *afford* it! Come on, man—there must be *billions* of dollars in taxes that are just *sitting* there!

• • • • •

Okay, now's your chance to explain to your second cousin why you would oppose that idea. Be sure to use both Biblical arguments *and* other reasonable explanations based on what you've learned. Jot down your ideas, and if you're in my in-person or online class, bring these ideas to our next class!

> **Take Quiz 9 (online or in-person students only).**
> **Feel free to use your notes, but there is a time limit!**
> **NOTE: You have 20 questions on this last quiz, instead of 10, but more time to take it (30 minutes).**

14.1 – CLAIM: "We <u>Have</u> to Regulate Barbers!"

First, answer these questions:

- In Romans 13:4, what does God's Word say that rulers ought to be?
- In 1 Peter 2:13-14, what does the Bible say is a ruler's *true* purpose?
- In Jeremiah 22:3, whom does God say that rulers should deliver *"out of the hand of the oppressor"*?
- In Ezekiel 45:9, what does God's Word say governments are to *"remove"* and *"execute"*?

• • • • •

The Scenario: Driving home by yourself one night after attending a homeschool dance (as well as buying essential oils for Mom), you run out of gas on a lonely, unlighted road 12 miles from town. Realizing that you left your flip phone at the dance, you walk down the road to find help, and you eventually arrive at a spooky old house at the edge of the deep, dark woods.
Surrounding the house is a mist-covered cemetery.
Nobody answers when you ring the doorbell, so with a great effort, you manage to open the heavy, creaky door, walk around and find a cobweb-filled bedroom, and fall onto a big bed in a deep sleep.
But...suddenly at 3 AM, you gasp and bolt upright in bed, thinking you heard...some *noise*.
Then you realize...it *was* a noise!

Something *is making creepy scratching sounds on your back bedroom window—**a window looking right into the cemetery.***

You get out of bed, tiptoe silently to the window, slowly pull back a set of dusty curtains, and see...*some kind of terrifying* **creature** *at your window! It has a ghostly, pallid face, and it slowly, slowwwwly opens the window as it stares right into your eyes and reaches out its bony fingers toward you!*

•••••

...Soon after you come to, you look up and realize that it's just your college economics professor again. (He's been looking a little pale and sickly lately.[122]) When he sees that you've regained consciousness, he tells you this:

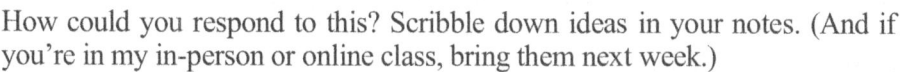

> Governments *have* to regulate professions like barbers. Officials should make them get licenses and take yearly classes. If they didn't, some barbers couldn't even cut hair properly. And some of them might even do something dangerous, like...I don't know...slice their customers' chins with their razors, or leave shaving cream on their faces until it burned their skin, or stick their fingers inside their mouths to turn their heads while they cut their hair!
>
> And anyway, don't I keep hearing all of you Christians claim that governments are supposed to protect others from harm and theft? If you really believed all that stuff you keep saying about government, you'd support mandatory licensing and training for barbers, so they wouldn't *harm* their customers!

•••••

How could you respond to this? Scribble down ideas in your notes. (And if you're in my in-person or online class, bring them next week.)

14.2 – Final Review, Part 1

If you're in my in-person or online Economics class, over the next two days you'll review for your final (to be taken on Day 14.4). The final is worth 200 points, and it covers material we've reviewed throughout the entire class. (Of course, if you're not in my in-person or online class, you can treat these last few pages as review material to wrap up the book.)

---

[122] And his fingers are pretty bony, too.

- Define **economics** and **steward**. How does knowing God's word and fearing Him make a person wise (1.1)?
- How do Christians live in some sense outside observable economics (1.2)?
- What does the Bible say are the proper duties of government? What two main mistakes does Henry Hazlitt say that bad economists make (1.3)?
- How does man's tendency to serve his *own* interests produce wealth for *others* in a voluntary-exchange economy (2.1)?
- Sum up a Christian view of wealth and riches (2.3).
- How does the Bible uphold the right to property (3.1)?
- Define **opportunity cost**, **scarcity**, **microeconomics**, and **macroeconomics**. What do Keynesian economists and Austrian economists believe (3.2)?
- Name several characteristics of gold and silver that make them useful for money (3.4).
- List some benefits of **profits** (4.2).
- Give the two false economic system choices of socialists/communists. How does Christian influence benefit a voluntary-exchange economy (4.3)?
- Define **socialism** and **communism**. List reasons why Christians should oppose them (4.4).
- Why is a centrally planned economy doomed to failure (5.1)?
- Sum up the "broken window fallacy" (5.4).
- Define **inflation**. What do some *mistakenly* believe inflation is? What three ways does government use to get money? How does inflation hurt the poor the worst? Why wouldn't everyone be rich if governments handed out millions of dollars to every single person (6.1, 6.2)?
- Define **interest**. How should interest rates be determined in a voluntary exchange economy? What do central banks cause when they artificially manipulate interest rates (6.3)?
- Review Tests 1 and 2.

14.3 – Final Review, Part 2

- How do supply and demand affect prices? Why should governments not interfere with prices? How could you argue that there's no such thing as "price gouging"? How does raising prices of high-demand items during an emergency make those items more available for those who need them (7.2)?
- What is the central message of "I, Pencil" (7.4)?
- Why do government spenders waste so much money (8.1)?

- Define **bureaucrat**. About what percent of all U. S. employees are bureaucrats? How does their pay compare to the average American's pay (8.2)?
- Explain the main point that Frederic Bastiat makes in "Public Works." What good question did Milton Friedman have about the public works project that he witnessed (8.3)?
- Give some examples of unintended consequences from bureaucrats' economic decisions. Why are bureaucrats much more likely to produce unintended consequences than private business owners (9.1)?
- Define **tariff**. How is a protective tariff an example of one of Henry Hazlitt's two basic economic mistakes? How do tariffs harm an economy? How are tariffs implemented not rationally or morally, but politically and sometimes corruptly (9.2)?
- Define **exaction**. What does God say about exactions? How do higher taxes harm an economy (10.1)?
- What does it reveal about economists and politicians who claim that saving money is harmful (10.2)?
- What effects do minimum wage laws have on an economy? Whom do they hurt the worst? What's the main factor that leads to higher wages, and how do governments slow this down (11.1)?
- Name some desirable skills and traits employers look for. What does Colossians 3:24-25 say about our work (11.2)?
- Define **strike** and **strikebreaker**. Why should a Christian be cautious about joining a labor union (11.3)?
- Sum up the common lesson of "The Rich and the Poor: A Fairy Tale" and the "Luxury Tax Myth" article (12.3, 13.3).
- Explain why you should never walk into a potentially haunted house and fall asleep, especially with your bedroom window unlocked (14.1).[123]
- Review Tests 3 and 4.

14.4 – Test 5 (Final)

In-person and online students, take Test 5, your cumulative final, today! Review your notes and tests (and the 14.2 & 14.3 review questions) once more if needed, focusing on the concepts that we've learned. The final is 40 questions, and it is worth 200 points. Do your very best!

---

[123] On second thought, just forget that one.

What Kingdom Are *You* a Part Of?

I hope you've enjoyed our look at economics! I pray that you got a little bit of a different perspective on that topic, based on a Christian worldview, which is also just and sensible.

It's too bad that governments won't confine themselves to doing what the Bible says are their moral, proper functions, or leave people alone to pursue their economic well-being. But what helps me to *not* despair, even though governments—including America's—do so many awful things? It's this:

> *I'm not expecting a perfect life here on earth, living under a perfectly just government. There are better things coming.*

Does it overwhelm you to realize that *any* government you live under will unjustly tax, control, and otherwise deal with you? Here's the best way you can possibly deal with it:

> *Become a citizen of the kingdom of God.*

Our sins separate us from God, though. The Bible teaches us that *"all have sinned, and come short of the glory of God" (Romans 3:23)*. But there is good news! God made a way for us to be forgiven of our sins: by placing them upon Jesus when He died on a cross. The Bible says that God *"made him [Jesus] to be sin for us, who knew no sin; that we might be made the righteousness of God in him" (2 Corinthians 5:21)*.

Being a nice person isn't enough. Being homeschooled isn't enough. Going to church isn't enough. It's only through Jesus Christ that you can get right with God. Jesus says this:

> *"I am the way, the truth, and the life: no man cometh unto the Father, but by me" (John 14:6).*

The Bible says that there is no other name except Jesus by whom we can be saved from our sins (Acts 4:12), and that there is only *"one mediator [go-between] between God and man, the man Christ Jesus; who gave himself a ransom for all" (1 Timothy 2:5-6)*.

So how do you have your sins forgiven and make peace with God—and have a life with Him after you die? The Bible says this:

> *"[I]f thou shalt confess with thy mouth the Lord Jesus, and shalt believe in thine heart that God hath raised him from the dead, thou shalt be saved" (Romans 10:9).*

When a Roman jailer asked the apostle Paul and his assistant Silas what he had to do to be saved from his sins, they told him this:

> *"Believe on the Lord Jesus Christ, and thou shalt be saved" (Acts 16:31).*

→

If you've never put your faith in Jesus Christ, do so right away! You don't have to say exactly the right words or change your ways first. Call out to God and ask Him to forgive your sins and save you through Jesus Christ.

Find a Bible-believing church and get an old Authorized Version ("King James") Bible and start reading the book of John.

And if you have any questions or need prayer about anything, feel free to email me any time: scott@homeschoolpartners.net.

Many blessings,
Scott Clifton

Did you enjoy this book?

If you did, I would be extremely grateful if you'd leave a brief review on Amazon.com!

It's fast and easy to leave a review! Here's how:

- Just do a search for "Economics for Christian Homeschoolers" at Amazon.com, and
- Hit "Ctrl+F" (for "Find") and type in "Write a customer review."

Thank you so much!
Scott Clifton

FREE Saxon Math® Online Video Lessons!

Using Saxon Math for your homeschooler? Would you like your student to have FREE, easy-to-follow, and FUN video lessons with practice problems worked out? Then check out my Saxon Math video lessons! Here's what you get:

- Simplified steps for students to copy down and use (different from the books!)

- Tips/tricks to make learning easier

- Practice problems worked out in detail

- A sense of humor to help "I hate math!" students relax and not pull out their hair in clumps

Check out the FREE video lessons below!

homeschoolpartners.net/math

Homeschool Humor

Do you like to laugh? (For example, "Ha, ha!")

Would you like to feel much better about your family's weird homeschooling experiences, since the ones in these books are even loonier?

Are you interested in soft, luxurious, and more manageable hair?

If you happened to answer "Yes" to any of those questions, *Homeschool Humor* books can help! (Except for the one about the soft, luxurious hair; maybe you should try egg whites or something.)

The two volumes of *Homeschool Humor* are packed with hilarious stories of the pitfalls and wackiness occurring in a somewhat-normal homeschool family, including chapters like...

- Let's Go Camping! Some Other Time!
- Naming Your Homeschooled Child
- Helping Your Children Build Strong Character by Smashing People Right in the Face
- Science and Other Mythical Creatures
- A Brief History of Homeschooling That Briefly Shows Homeschooling Throughout History, in a Brief Way That Is Also Historical

Also included: juicy lists of how to answer those complete strangers who ask, "Are those all your children?" or "What are those kids doing out of school?"

Homeschool Humor books are available here:

homeschoolpartners.net/books

7th–12th Grade Literature for Christian Homeschoolers:

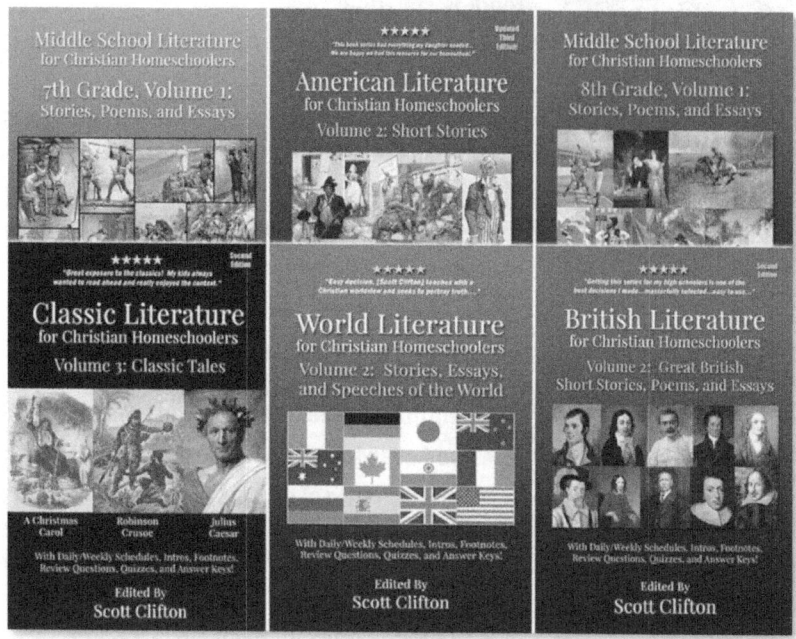

Here's what you get with the above sets of literature books for Christian middle school and high school homeschoolers:

- **Great Reads!** Many wonderful essays, short stories, speeches, poems, letters, and novels—in conveniently arranged sets for seventh grade, eighth grade, and four years of high school.

- **A 30-Week, Four-Days-Per-Week Reading Schedule.** No more asking, "What should we read this week?"

- **Introductions, Footnotes, Questions for Review.** These place writings into historical context, help students understand archaic terms, clear up potentially hazy passages, and help the student think about important ideas.

- **A Christian Worldview.** This worldview is reflected in the introductions, footnotes, and review questions.

- **Free Answer Keys to Review Questions.** Parents, you can discuss the review questions—fully armed with answer keys!

homeschoolpartners.net/books

American Government & Politics: A Christian Worldview

- A helpful, 30-week, two-to-four-day-per-week reading schedule
- A good overview of American Government, in clear, short sections
- A Christian view of government and government types, the Constitution and how to interpret it, political parties, taxes, and more
- Review questions for each day's reading
- Free review question answer key

Civics for Christian Homeschoolers

- A helpful, 15-week, four-day-per-week schedule
- A good overview of Civics, in clear, short sections
- A Christian view of citizenship, types of law, types of government, the Declaration of Independence, a Christian's rights and responsibilities, juries, voting, and more
- Review questions for each day's reading
- Free review question answer key

Economics for Christian Homeschoolers

- A helpful, 14-week, four-day-per-week schedule
- Clear, short sections
- A Christian view of economics, with a pro-free market viewpoint
- Explanations of the dangers of socialism, inflation, bureaucracies, taxes and business regulations, and other government meddling
- Review questions for each day's reading
- Free review question answer key

homeschoolpartners.net/books

About Scott Clifton

North Carolina is where Scott Clifton makes his home, with his wife Julie and their children. Scott is a fervent homeschooling advocate, and just *seconds* after his first child was born, as he took his little baby boy and held him close to his chest, he looked down and immediately knew—right then in his heart—that he would never be able to wear that particular shirt again. (Also, that he and Julie would homeschool their children, which they have done since 1994.)

Scott earned his B.A. in Journalism from the University of Central Florida and his M.Ed. from York University. He began his career writing and editing for a family newspaper and a state banking association. In 2002, the Lord led Scott into the field of home school education, and that year he began teaching classes full time as the owner and operator of Home School Partners (**homeschoolpartners.net**).

Made in the USA
Coppell, TX
11 March 2026